I'M QUIRKY

I'M QUIRKY

**just weird enough to be intriguing,
but not enough to repel!**

*Special thanks to Magi Sloan for all of her constructive
criticism, guidance and encouragement.*

© John MacCalman, 2021

Published by John MacCalman

For more information, e-mail all enquiries to
maccalman@hotmail.com
www.maccalman.com

A CIP catalogue record for this book is available from the British
Library.

ISBN 978-1-9989944-0-3

Book layout and design by Clare Brayshaw

Cover design by Matthew C. Howe

Prepared and printed by:

York Publishing Services Ltd
64 Hallfield Road
Layerthorpe
York YO31 7ZQ

Tel: 01904 431213

Website: www.yps-publishing.co.uk

Contents

Music Producer Clark Sorley from Kilmarnock on a whirlwind trip around the USA
It was not surprising that the airline went bust shortly after this

Making music for TV, Radio and Movies at just the right length
The True Love Orchestra – Wedding Song for Sarah Ferguson and HRH Prince Andrew. Producing records with Craig Ferguson in the guise of Bing Hitler, and noted actors Alan Cumming and Forbes Masson in their comedy act Victor and Barry
Movie music success in the USA

Dangerous fireworks at a midnight open-air concert
Loyalty to individuals on management contracts when they go solo

Attempts to get record deals
Los Angeles attorney hired
Madam Wong's West is not a brothel!
Foggy Bottom is not something you get from a strong curry!

Creating Stick it in Your Ear!
Hoovered at the Albany Hotel at 3am – T shirts
Supercharge song story "She Moved the Dishes First"
Programme series "Hear Me Talking" – without the interviewer
Award winning production The Big Day

How to win as a frequent flyer

About the Author

John was born in a big house next to Scotstounhill railway station, Glasgow, Scotland on 2nd of July 1947. He attended Hillhead High School but was expelled in the 6th year for truancy, as he preferred to spend his time at Scottish TV studios watching the production of their live lunchtime show *The One O'clock Gang.*

His early railway influences resulted in an 8-year employment with British Rail (BR) after leaving school. BR put him through a 2-year course in Business Studies at the Central College of Commerce and Distribution in Glasgow as part of a Railway Studentship scheme.

His enthusiasm for broadcasting had met with a major obstacle in finding a career entry point due to lack of experience, so he, along with a couple of friends started Radio Phoenix broadcasting to Forresthall Geriatric Hospital in Glasgow on a weekly basis.

The *Sound Broadcasting Act of 1972* presented the major opportunity for him with the commercial radio franchise for Glasgow being awarded to Radio Clyde. He was fortunate enough to join the pioneering team as a Production Assistant in November 1973.

During his 34 years at Radio Clyde he became Production Controller, produced many award winning programmes, created the Kelvingrove Free Music Festivals and organised live broadcasts from the USA. He acted as Travel Editor taking opportunity to experience many overseas destinations. His enthusiasm for aviation resulted in several documentaries on the subject including "*Tales from Kai Tak*" about Hong Kong's old airport.

Parallel to this he became interested in the local music scene and formed Publishing and Management Companies to develop local talent. He travelled frequently to the USA West Coast ending up with Million Mile status on Northwest Airlines.

In 2007 he was made redundant by Bauer Media, the new owners of Radio Clyde, and took a year out to research a ten-part proposed TV series on aviation in Micronesia. This featured Air Mike – the Island Hopper at that time part of Continental Airlines.

In 2008 he joined Travel 2 as a Sales Consultant advising UK Travel Agents on worldwide travel. As part of this job he travelled to Australia and New Zealand many times. In addition, he had a love of casinos as well as flying. So frequent trips were made to Las Vegas, and Australian cities like Melbourne, Sydney, Perth, Brisbane, Perth and Cairns.

In November 2020 he took voluntary redundancy from Travel 2 and now works freelance consulting and writing.

Chapter 1

Expelled

Driving a steam train at the age of 8.
Bad boy activities.
Corporal punishment.
Expelled from school.

I was conceived on a night sleeper train between Glasgow and London in October 1946. Well, that's what one of my sisters told me and while she may have been kidding, it would account for my love of trains. I was born in Glasgow on July 2, 1947, in a big house with a large garden next to Scotstounhill Railway Station. This was to have an early influence on my first job! As a kid, I grew up among steam trains and would often be found down at the station helping the stationmaster who would later assist me secure a full-time job. There was a small coal depot close to the station and at the age of eight, I experienced driving my first and only steam locomotive when the engineer invited me up to the footplate. He then held me up so I could pull the regulator to power the locomotive. I would from an early age lend a hand to the station staff and collect tickets from passengers.

John's Scotstounhill Home

I loved the garden as a playground and as a source of fantastic ideas like trying to dig a tunnel to Australia! I was fond of the trams which ran outside our door that were my transport for the three mile journey to school. I joined the Boy Scouts which at that time for me was a great adventure. I wasn't by any means an angel child. I would do crazy things like set fire to toilet paper in the pan just to watch it burn. It did and melted part of the seat! One evening I was once encouraged in an act of vandalism by a local gang to pour cement through the shutters of the shop just across the road from our house. I left a track of footprints in white cement dust right to our front door so even Inspector Clouseau could track down the suspect! The police duly arrived but thankfully, the shop declined to press charges, as they seemed to know that some bad boys had put me up to it.

Growing up as a teenager in the Sixties was great. I had two half sisters who were ten and eleven years older than I was. My father had married again after his first wife died leaving him to care for two small girls. My first interests in broadcasting came from my older sister Pat who worked as a news secretary at BBC TV in Queen Margaret Drive, Glasgow. Every evening she would come home with stories about "what went wrong today."

My parents were both working so quite often I would have to fend for myself and at an early age I picked up the rudiments of cooking.

My sister Rosemary attended the College of Domestic Science in Glasgow and, after qualifying, she took a job in charge of the "dinner ladies" at Clydebank High School. A common dish at that time for the kids was minced beef. Rosemary discovered to her horror that the preparation of the dish by the cooks involved boiling up a vat of water then throwing in a massive quantity of raw meat that produced a horrible rubbery dish to serve. She taught them how to brown the mince before adding the water and the kids loved it.

She didn't stay too long in catering as she had studied Spanish and managed to get a job as a courier representative for holiday tour operator Thompsons in Spain. Her Spanish friend Rosamaria Pardo Pelaz – would come over to visit and they would go out in Glasgow pretending both to be Spanish not speaking any English. They had great fun when men tried to chat them up and of course the guys didn't realise they could understand every word they were saying, especially to each other about what they were going to do with the girls!

I wasn't happy at school. I went to Hillhead High where I think they were more interested in making up quotas than meeting any educational desires of the pupils. I was very interested in Geography so they made me drop it in favour of History. Corporal punishment ruled and I would frequently receive "the belt". The official name for this was the tawse, which consisted of a strip of leather with one end split into a number of tails. It was used to punish pupils of either sex on the palm of the outstretched hand held palm uppermost supported by the other hand to make it difficult to move away during the infliction of strokes. After two Scottish mothers went to the European Court of Human Rights in 1982, the practice eventually became banned by law in the UK.

When I sought out careers advice, they hadn't a clue about broadcasting which was my passion mainly due to my sister's influence from her work at the BBC. I started to skip days at school and would often go up to the studios of Scottish Television in Cowcaddens and watch them make the live lunchtime show *The One O'Clock Gang*. I even appeared on the show once when Gerry Marsden of Gerry and the Pacemakers was a guest artiste. This was a bit risky because I could have been found out playing truant. This became a rather bad habit and my absences were so frequent that halfway through 6th Year they made my absence permanent – I was expelled!

Chapter 2

Pirate Radio

Failed audition for pirate radio station – Radio Scotland.
Billy Connolly encounter.
BBC script rejection from
That Was The Week That Was.

In 1965, the Pirate Radio Station, Radio Scotland was all the rage. My late father, Hugh Turner MacCalman, was a lawyer who mainly specialised in licensing work but one of his clients was Mr T.V. Shields who had created Radio Scotland so naturally I wanted to become a DJ or at least work in the medium. I actually did an audition for Radio Scotland supervised by Brian Holden, a rather stern South African who was in charge at their Cranworth Street Studios in Glasgow. There were several hopefuls present, and the audition included reading a rather tough news script and describing an object talking constantly for one minute making sense. It is harder than you may think! It was the time of the Vietnam War. The news item contained some foreign names, among them was Nguyen Cao Ky, Prime Minister of South Vietnam. One DJ hopeful decided to call him Mr Hoochie-Coochie. He didn't get the job. Neither did I!

I also took up the guitar rather badly and formed a band that did not last very long – the Spectre Beat Unit. We did about three gigs before I realised it wasn't for me. I reckoned that I had played the guitar and lost! One of the gigs was at Jordanhill Teacher Training College. Playing at the same venue that night was a young Billy Connolly.

I had an attempt at TV scriptwriting in 1963 that earned me my first rejection letter from the BBC! It was for the late night satire show hosted by David Frost, *"That Was The Week That Was"*, and the subject of my script was a political party's leadership election. I wrote in the style of a horse race commentary with each contender taking part in the race. I reckon my horse fell at the first fence.

Chapter 3

1965 to 1973 British Rail, Hospital Broadcasting and Israel

Religious bigotry in Glasgow.
Jewish girlfriend and trip to Israel.
If you can't get in to broadcasting then start
your own radio station.

The early influence of growing up beside the railway station paid off in my search for employment. Thanks to a recommendation from the stationmaster at Scotstounhill in the summer of 1965, I joined British Railways in Glasgow Central Station Enquiry Office dealing with the public.

I remember well the job interview. It was at the Divisional HQ of British Railways, 87 Union Street, Glasgow on the 6th Floor in Room 9 which had on the door, not surprisingly, Room 69. Some wag had the number 1 scrawled on in front of the 6 and a 0 after the 9. For the mathematically challenged, that changed the number to room 1690 which apparently has some historical significance being the anniversary of the Battle of the Boyne. I was not one to take sides in the Protestant vs Catholics bigotry prevalent in the city at that time. In fact when challenged as a teenager by the gangs around Scotstoun as to what football team I supported to see which way I was inclined (Rangers for Protestant or Celtic for Catholic), I chose an alternate of Queens Park – an amateur team. They would laugh at me and I avoided a beating. The interview started with what school did you attend? I passed that when I said Hillhead High as it certainly wasn't a Catholic School. They then gave me a massive tome, the British Railways Timetable, to look at and then asked me questions about train times. I was such a nerd that I could respond without looking up the timetable!

That launched an 8-year career that I did enjoy. I started at Glasgow Central Station Inquiry Office at the public counter or on the telephone at what must have been an early call centre in an area at the back. The attitude of the management went against my natural instinct to be helpful. We were told never to write things down for customers, as they would hold it against us if anything was wrong. I remember early on being told off for giving out too much information! A customer asked why there was no train service between Wemyss Bay and Largs, a distance of around 8 miles. I knew my history of the area and explained that a landowner on the route refused permission for a railway to be built. That was too much information!

After Glasgow Central I was the booking clerk at Hillfoot Station in Bearsden then went on to a two-year Railway Studentship course spending time at Falkirk Grahamston Goods Station, Motherwell Central and the Divisional HQ in Union Street. There was a section in the HQ called Work Study and one of the clerks spent most of the time sleeping at his desk. Every time I saw him, I found myself humming the Herman's Hermans hit of the time "Sleepy Joe". After that, I ended up in the Greenock Area Manager's Office for four years. There was a delightful hostelry next to the station called the Trades Hotel which, to put it quite crudely, was a licensed doss house located in Bogle Street and known locally as "*The Bogle*". To supplement my income I would occasionally take a job on the door of this establishment as a bouncer. At that point in my life I would have probably qualified for the role of the seven stone scrawny weakling in the adverts for body-building in the style of Charles Atlas. So this was a bit incongruous due to my limited stature. Could that be The Stature of Limitations? Later in life I was to put on sufficient weight to be a daunting prospect for camels. More on that later.

I also had my first venture into pop promotion. I would spend weekends down at Millport on the Isle of Cumbrae doing a DJ spot at the dance hall in the Garrison. When in Glasgow my Saturday nights consisted of a visit to Bearsden Burgh Hall where they had a dance with live bands. One of these bands was Tony Rivers and the Castaways who did an excellent job of covering Beach Boys hits as well as their own songs. I thought it would be great to put them on in Millport so I booked them and paid up front. They were great but the gig was a financial disaster.

My parents had many friends in the Jewish Community and helped out an organisation known as The Bridge in Britain. This set up visits to the UK for Israeli students by providing them with accommodation and board with a family for a couple of weeks. In the summer of 1969, our house was host to a young sabra Israeli girl, Michal Lowenstein. Sabra is a term for a person born in Israel. We fell for each other big style and this was my first true love encounter at the age of 22! When she returned to Israel, we kept in touch and I decided to go out to the Land of Milk and Honey to see Michal in November 1969.

I flew from London with EL AL and experienced their intense security. Michal stayed in Haifa but I had chosen a hotel just outside the city. We were trying to rekindle the relationship we had in Scotland, but there were a couple of major obstacles. Her parents were of Germanic Jewish stock and could not understand how I had come out all the way to Israel but had no interest in visiting the holy sites in Jerusalem. The fact that I was not Jewish didn't help. They suspected that I was after only one thing, their daughter! We had no opportunity to be really intimate, and so on my last night we were resigned to the impossibility of continuing this long distance love affair. I returned to the UK and she went into the Israeli Army.

While all that was going on, I was still very keen on developing my broadcasting interests. Any time I tried to secure a job in the industry I was met with "you have to have experience" therefore, what better way was there than to start my own radio station? I met up with some like-minded people who were also very keen on the notion and we decided to try to establish a Hospital Radio service in Glasgow with the name Radio Phoenix. Two key friends in this project were Bob Carson and Irene Craney.

When we were looking for volunteers for Radio Phoenix we put an advert in the Glasgow Herald for a new kind of radio service. Bob Carson and I borrowed my father's law office in Hope Street for interviews with prospective presenters. Among those who turned up were Dave Marshall and Tiger Tim Stevens!

We had dreams of setting up a big network serving all the Glasgow hospitals so we approached the authorities with our ideas. Naturally, we planned on a pop music type service.

It was the Glasgow Northern Board of Management that saw in our approach something that was desperately needed but not in the form we had been thinking. Foresthall Hospital and Home in Springburn was a geriatric care establishment filled with lonely neglected old people. They offered us a trial period of one year to provide a weekly programme service for a couple of hours over the relay system in the hospital every Sunday. Their wisdom in giving us this challenge was probably the best thing that ever happened to my ambitions.

It was a major culture shock to me and the rest of the team. We built up a music library not of current pop hits but of very oldies – traditional Scottish, wartime hits and standards. We went round the wards making a great effort to talk to the patients. For many of them, we were the only visitors they ever had and it was tough going. At the end of the year, we were honoured by the Hospital Board with a special dinner and their grateful thanks. For me it was a great lesson on how to succeed by listening to your listeners.

Radio Phoenix was the pilot scheme out of which grew HBS (Hospital Broadcasting Service) Glasgow serving several hospitals in the city. While that developed, Bob Carson and I were both still very keen to enter the broadcasting industry on a professional basis.

I also ventured into a morsel of pirate radio in 1972 under a fictitious name as I did not want to jeopardise my chances of a legitimate career. Radio Free Scotland had been a land based pirate operation as an unofficial arm of the Scottish National Party (SNP) broadcasting infrequently from 1956 to 1972. It started by using the sound on the BBC TV channel after closedown. In 1970 they switched their operations from the TV sound channel to radio, broadcasting on 260 metres on the medium wave band with an ambitious 3 hour presentation every Sunday.

In 1972 I had discovered Radio Free Scotland by accident but I thought their programmes were to put it bluntly – crap; lacking entertainment value. I reckoned I could do much better so I sent off demo tape to them under the stage name of John Douglas. I heard nothing for about 3 weeks when out of the blue they broadcast my demo tape! Shortly afterwards they got in touch and said the delay was due to the fact that my demo was so good they thought it was someone from the government/detector van service trying to infiltrate their organisation!

For several weeks I did a regular music show for them on tape but with no politics from me – I left that to them as at that time I had no particular political leanings. It came time for the SNP party conference to be held in Rothesay on the Isle of Bute and they decided to set up a radio station for the duration. They booked a wee boarding house in Rothesay where we were to set up a clandestine studio. We thought we would have to keep it secret from the landlady but while we were setting up the equipment and trying to rig the antenna outside her husband came in and suggested we use the washing line as it would send out a better signal! They also had an arrangement with the Calmac Ferries that if a detector van was spotted on the mainland boarding the ship, they would let us know and give us time to shut down.

That was to be my last venture into pirate radio as a legitimate career beckoned.

Chapter 4

Radio Clyde December 1973

Pioneering radio days.
Two months before the start of
commercial radio in Scotland.

The Sound Broadcasting Act of 1972 was my big opportunity. This legislation changed the Independent Television Authority (ITA) into the Independent Broadcasting Authority (IBA) and set about establishing commercial radio in the UK. Glasgow was one of the first areas to be identified as a site for one of the new radio stations and the IBA carried out "public consultation" as to what listeners in the area wanted from the radio station. Bob Carson and I, with tireless help from Irene Craney, set about preparing a written submission to the IBA with our thoughts. We handed it in to them and it was kindly acknowledged. Then the wheels of the Authority started to move in my favour by presenting a great opportunity.

The Royal Television Society (RTS) was holding an event in Glasgow about the future of commercial radio. By this time the Glasgow franchise had almost been finalised and Jimmy Gordon, later Lord Gordon of Strathblane, who headed the company which had been successful, was going to address the event. The IBA arranged that I would have the chance to address the gathering on "the listeners' attitude to commercial radio". What was more important to me was that I would have the chance to meet Jimmy Gordon.

We frantically set about preparing a proposed programme schedule on how we would run a commercial station. Bob Carson at this point had succeeded in his career ambitions and was now working for Thames Television in London. The proposals I had were not for the RTS event but were for me to give to Jimmy Gordon.

When I look back at them now there were so many glaring errors in the schedule both in philosophy and practicality but despite these Jimmy Gordon shortly afterwards offered me a job as a Station Assistant. I joined the company two months before they went on air. I packed in my career with British Rail; after all it was just a change of station, and in November 1973 reported to the new HQ of Radio Clyde under construction in the Anderston Cross Centre in Glasgow.

Although Jimmy Gordon had hired me I was to work under Andy Park, Head of Entertainment, a remarkably appropriate title in so many ways as the years ahead were to unfold. In the role of Production Assistant, I was joined by Annie Wood.

These days you would probably be called a producer but that was a title frowned upon as being very BBC. As a Production Assistant (PA), your main job was to help put the programmes together. You would learn all about copyrights, music, artists, and relationships with record companies. It was all very new so we had to make it up as we went along.

John in the early Radio Clyde days

There's a fabulous book by Tony Currie who was the first DJ on air called *Not Quite Altogether Now* which goes into great detail about those pioneering days and I would highly recommend it. Consequently, I'll omit most material covered by Tony and only cover highlights and lowlights of the weird and wonderful world that was my time at Radio Clyde. In his book, Tony described me as *producer, presenter, technician and general dogsbody. John appeared to benefit from the rare talent of apparently surviving for lengthy periods without the need for sleep.* I'll examine in detail in Chapter 19 some of the highlights and lowlights of my almost 35 years at Radio Clyde.

In November and December of 1973, we spent much of our time contacting record companies to try to gain free supplies of their products and create awareness of our existence and how working together would be of mutual advantage. This proved to be quite difficult as the music industry was still very London centric and not tuned in to the potential that commercial radio offered them especially in such remote places as Scotland!

While most of the on air talent we recruited prior to our on air date was Scottish there was one major exception – Steve Jones who was born in England, Crewe to be precise. He was at that time working for BBC Radio 1. He had been the bass guitarist for Lonnie Donegan and had also formed his own band with the delightful name of *Hunt, Lunt and Cunningham!* He was the number one choice by Andy Park to host the mid-morning show. He was charming, friendly and had a wicked sense of humour. I was totally taken in by a story he told about his arrival in Glasgow and how he had received a blow job from the maid at his hotel along with his breakfast! He was so convincing in his delivery that I believed it till he came to the punch line. He said that as he was checking out that morning the manager asked him how he had enjoyed his stay. Steve had responded with the fact that it was wonderful but he was curious about the "extra" service he had received. The manager said, "Aha, that's simple. We were told by the tourist board that in order to get an extra star in our rating we would have to install a Goblin Teasmade in every room!"

There were to be three main live studios plus one for news presentation and a commercial production studio separate from the main area which could not go live. Studio A was equipped to be self-operated as well as with a guest area. In visual range was both Studio C which could be self-operated or as a control room and the News Studio. Separate from them was Studio B with a control room, multitrack recording desk and separate performance area which would be used for music and drama. As a Production Assistant, I had to learn how to operate all of the studio desks, as not all the presenters would be able to self-operate.

In this period, key presentation staff were hired, including Richard Park, Dave Marshall, and Tony Currie. Once Studio A was completed, they started to dummy run the shows.

Not everyone made it to the on-air date. One potential presenter found the strain too much. Just a few days prior to the on-air date, he headed out of the Production Office supposedly to do his show and instead of turning right to the studio, turned left and headed out the front door never to be seen again.

New Year's Eve 31st December 1973 at 10.30 pm was when Radio Clyde began broadcasting. My main duties that opening night were to man the studio phone-in equipment. In fact I came on shift at 9.00 pm and ended up working right through to 11.00 pm on the 1st of January either on desk operating for presenters or answering the phones. I did have breaks, but this tended to set the pattern for my years ahead in radio where it became quite natural to pull an all-nighter just to complete a production.

Working excessively long hours and through the night was the norm for quite a few staff members. When plans were drawn up ten years later for the station to move to its own purpose built premises in Clydebank, not only were two bedrooms included but also a swimming pool!

Much of the early months were spent recording programmes, operating the desk on live shows including news magazines and voicing commercials for which we were paid separately. In these early days, unlike in American radio, presenters were not allowed to voice commercials within their own shows as this was considered to be a form of endorsement. This became a nice little supplement to my annual salary which was £2,200.

Chapter 5

Pan Am Flights to Trinidad December 1975

First Class travel reward for radio work.
High powered executives steal the cutlery.
First and only attempt at a drug deal.
How radio in Trinidad was crudely relayed the
BBC World Service

In December 1975, Jimmy Gordon called me into his office and said, "You haven't had a real holiday since you joined us" (which was not quite true as I did have a break in October 1974). "We have a considerable amount of money which has to be taken in flights with Pan Am before the end of the year". This was known as "contra" whereby they would give us flights in exchange for advertising. There were some strange conditions attached to this. While I could fly anywhere in their worldwide network, I could only transit the USA, not stay there. I looked at their network and thought Christmas in the Caribbean would be brilliant. Big mistake! I chose Trinidad but to get there I would have to fly from London to Frankfurt, then Frankfurt to New York's Kennedy Airport (JFK) and on to Port of Spain. Flying home would be straightforward, so I thought, a simple connection from Port of Spain to JFK and on to London Heathrow.

I was concerned that my chosen itinerary was going to cost more than there was in the contra account so I asked Jimmy Gordon how much we had and he replied "enough"! It turned out that as it was Christmas season the outbound flights were only available in First Class. What a hardship! The return would be in Economy and in those days I was happy just to be flying.

On December 18th I went to London Heathrow where I was to pick up my ticket on departure. It took the desk agent half an hour to write out the complex paper ticket for the itinerary. There were a total of five flight coupons on self-carbonating paper but you had to lean hard on your pen to make sure the copies were all legible. He had to put in the individual tax breakdown on each ticket for each sector. Electronic tickets were years in the future.

Check in completed I had time for a brief visit to the lounge before boarding the short hop to Frankfurt then board the Pan Am 747 for the 3,849-mile trip to New York's JFK Airport. Pan Am's 747 was configured with First Class up front on the main deck and a spiral staircase leading upstairs to the dining area in the bubble reserved exclusively for their premium passengers in First.

A couple of hours into the flight a steward approached and asked if I would care to join them upstairs for luncheon. In the upstairs bubble there were two sets of four elegantly dressed tables. I was placed alongside three rather high-powered guys. One was a vice president of Ford who had been out to resolve a labour dispute at their German plant. The other two were equally high-ranking entrepreneurs returning home for Christmas. While the meal was outstanding what surprised me was the manner in which my fellow travellers were surreptitiously pocketing items of silverware all embossed "Pan Am" as souvenirs of their trip. I was the last to leave the table but before I did I mentioned to the steward the kleptomania customs of my companions at the table. He replied, "on the money they are paying for their tickets we can afford it!"

On arrival in New York my connection was so tight that I was escorted to the gate for my Boeing 727 flight down to Port of Spain. I made it but my bag didn't so when I hit Trinidad – no bag, but it was delivered to my hotel the next day. The hotel was pretty quiet and the weather was lousy as it was the rainy season. I was totally bored.

I took a walk around the streets of Port of Spain when I was presented with the opportunity to do my first and only drug deal. "Hey man, would you like to buy some weed. We got it ready-rolled. Only $40TT (approx $20) for a pack."

It was the 70s and while I had sampled weed and on one occasion coke, I wasn't by any means a regular user but it struck me that it would be cool to have some to pass the time as the place seemed pretty uninspiring. So I said OK. He asked me for the money which I readily handed over.

He said, "Wait here and I'll just go and get the smokes for you!" I wasn't aware that I radiated so much simplicity but there must have been some illuminated sign saying "mug for the taking". I'm still waiting for him to come back with the goods!

I'd come out to Trinidad to escape from the world of broadcasting, but after a couple of days I felt I should pay a courtesy call on the local radio station, NBS Radio 610 which was government owned and part of Trinidad and Tobago Television TTTV. It was late morning and the presenter on air invited me into the studio which was a pretty old-fashioned set up. The microphone he was using was one of these large rectangular shaped devices that looked so old BBC Bush House. Across from his presentation table was an old radio set. He announced to his listeners "It's time now for de news from de BBC in London". He grabbed the large microphone, reached across to the radio and turned it up thrusting the device in front of the speaker. That was how they relayed the BBC World Service!

On Boxing Day 1975 I was scheduled to fly back with Pan Am from Port of Spain via JFK to London but the flight from Port of Spain for the 2213 mile trip to New York was running several hours late so I missed my connection. In those days most airlines would actually give you overnight accommodation and put you on the next available flight. The only snag was I didn't have a Visa for the USA. To cover circumstances like this it's called "Transfer Without Visa" where the airline would land the passenger in the USA and take responsibility for them to ensure they left on the next available flight. They gave me a hotel voucher and I had my first experience of a New York Airport hotel which was sad to say quite unmemorable! Next morning it was back to London in economy on the daytime flight and then an overnight sleeper train back to Glasgow.

Little did I know then that this experience of First Class travel was just a taste of many more flights to come.

Chapter 6

SuperScoreboard Secrets

How a radio guru creatively produced an image
of predictive powers at football matches

In radio, the words create the pictures for the listeners. What the listener can't see is painted in their minds by the commentators. The guru of sports presentation on Radio Clyde was Richard Park, the creator of the Scoreboard formats, who in partnership with journalist Jimmy Sanderson, had the ability to make predictions with remarkable accuracy, so it seemed to the audience.

One outstanding example of this creativity I witnessed was when I was the Production Assistant on a Glasgow Rangers home game at Ibrox Stadium. Richard and Jimmy were doing their pre-match scene-set from the commentary box. As was the practice, members of the press shortly before kickoff would be given the team sheets listing all the players, positions and also reserves for each side. Without revealing the fact that they had already been given the team sheets, Richard would ask Jimmy for his "predictions" for today's line up. So, with uncanny accuracy Jimmy was able in the listener's mind to predict the full line up occasionally throwing in one error to avoid suspicion.

At one point during the run of SuperScoreboard Radio Clyde lost the rights to live commentary from the grounds when the BBC spent big money on exclusivity. We were limited to a set number of time constraint live flashes from around the grounds. To create atmosphere in the studio I had recorded from several locations what we would call a wild-track sound effect of the atmosphere at the grounds. While Richard hosted the studio-bound show, we would run the sound effect to give the impression we were live at a ground somewhere. We had to be careful that we didn't use anything with partisan singing in the background.

Richard had the remarkable instinct of being able to go to a ground just when a goal was being scored. This was aided by us recording each of the grounds' inputs in the studio so if we did miss one live, we could then go to it minutes later "as live". If you've ever watched Sky Sports NFL Red Zone with Scott Hanson you'll understand the method.

Within Radio Clyde I moved on to become Production Co-ordinator and then in July 1981 Production Controller. This was at the same time that Richard Park became a very successful Music Controller.

Chapter 7

Into the Music Business

*My dislike of The Waltons on TV launches
my ventures into the music business.
Setting up two publishing and management companies –
Jammy Music and Scotia Nostra.
Devious publicity stunt banning a singer from
getting married.
Unexpected success from two customs officers.*

By the time I joined Radio Clyde I had moved into my own flat in Grantley Street in the Shawlands area of Glasgow's South Side not far from the a bar called the Doune Castle. One evening I was sitting at home and *The Waltons* came on the TV. I couldn't stand them so I figured "I'm off out for a drink". I wandered into the Doune Castle and I heard music coming from the cellar downstairs.

A band was playing so I sat down and started to enjoy them however I didn't recognise any of their songs. Their front man, Billy Fairbairn, had a great rapport with the audience. If someone in the band broke a string, he would fill the time while it was changed with George Carlin routines! At half time I approached them and asked them "how much of your own material do you do?", "All of it is our own" was the slightly miffed reply. I was impressed and my love affair with *Underhand Jones* was born.

I figured that I could help them with my contacts in the music business through Radio Clyde however I would have to keep any activity separate to avoid any conflict of interest. With a friend, Andrew Harvey, who was a successful Chartered Accountant interested in some kind of involvement in the music business, we formed two Limited Companies to look after the interests of the band. One was Jammy Music Publishers Ltd. and the other was Scotia Nostra Management Ltd. We signed up the band members Billy Fairbairn and Campbell (Cammy) Forbes, to the publishing company and the whole band to the management deal. The band owned their own small PA system and Cammy's kid brother Keith Forbes – known as "big Ski" for reasons that escape me – operated the PA system.

There were many interesting pub venues in and around Glasgow which featured live music but I loved The Amphora in Sauchiehall Street best because it had the most perfect room for live performance. I'm sure Big Ski would tell you. The room was carpeted and the wall very non-reflective of sound so playing at a sensible level you could get an excellent PA mix throughout.

When the band's lead singer Billy Fairbairn told me he was getting married my reaction was that this would not be good for the band to have the front man "unavailable" to his female fans. I then sensed an opportunity to make the best out of a bad situation and get some free publicity for the band. I took Billy into my confidence on what I planned so when the press came knocking on his door he would play along. The scheme was to leak to the press that I had banned Billy from getting married under the terms of his management contract with Scotia Nostra Management Ltd. This stated that he could not enter into any other contract without my express written permission, and his marriage would be a contract. When I got a call from a reporter from the Daily Record, I acted very angry and swore down the phone. I could feel the reporter's excitement as he reckoned he had a great story. The next day the story appeared with the headline "Billy in Wedding Ban" and a picture of him with his bride to be. Needless to say I relented and let the wedding go ahead. He hadn't told me that she was heavily pregnant at the time but the Daily Record photographer who took the picture said they had to be careful to make sure the pregnancy was not on display as it may have offended some of their readers. My, how times have changed!

A photographer did come to our aid once to save Campbell Forbes from losing his driving licence. He had parked the band's van outside The Amphora and while they were setting up the equipment inside, a rather nasty police sergeant came in and charged him with parking the van so as to cause an obstruction. It was too close the pedestrian crossing lights. When the formal charge came through with a court appearance required, I noticed it claimed he had parked between a line of studs on the road and the actual crossing which was an offence. I reckoned that there were no studs clearly marked so I got Ronnie Anderson, an excellent photographer, to take some photos which clearly showed the absence of studs. I then wrote to the Procurator Fiscal to advise that this would be our defence. The charge was dropped.

One outstanding gig for Underhand Jones was The Loch Lomond Rock Festival in June 1980. I knew the promoter, John Caulfield, and was able to secure the band an early short 20-minute spot. While they were playing the stage manager told me that the next band had been delayed and would be late reaching the stage. He asked if Underhand Jones could play a longer set. I passed the word on to the boys and they duly obliged. They'd probably have played all day if given the chance. In true professional style they made no hint to any backstage problems and played longer till the word came that the next band had arrived. Unfortunately this may have backfired on them because some of the crowd thought that the band had deliberately overrun their slot.

Underhand Jones broke up late 1980 and Cammy Forbes and Brian Coyle went on to form *The Dolphins*. Despite investing heavily, we never made any money out of Underhand Jones.

Scotia Nostra Management was eventually wound up but Jammy Music did have some successes from other projects.

Jammy Music had been formed to look after Underhand Jones and initially I hadn't thought of expanding into other artists until two Customs Officers came to see me about a song they had written. They heard I was a music publisher and they had a Scottish song that they wanted published. I explained that I was really only interested in the pop market but I would give it a listen.

The song was "Always Argyll" and I could hear it had potential. In fact all I could hear was the sound of a cash register going ka-ching at the end of each line. I signed it up and placed it with music producer Pete Shipton who was working on a new album for Scots singer Valerie Dunbar who just happened to be his wife. He liked it and it became the title song of her new album. It was my first success as a publisher and the song went on to have more than 30 covers from other artistes worldwide.

There was a great story about one of these covers that came out under the title "Always Mayo". An Irish record company wanted to use the song but change the lyrics. To do this they must have the permission of the original publisher. They wanted a 30% share in the royalties of the adapted version which would have been a reasonable request except for the fact that they had already produced the album without first obtaining permission. We granted permission but without their 30% share!

Chapter 8

Kelvingrove Festivals

*Establishment of free open-air rock festivals
in Glasgow for bands with original music.*

R adio Clyde was very much community based.
Managing Director Jimmy Gordon recognised how
much the listeners had contributed to the success of the
station and wanted to give something back by way of a
thank you. In 1976 the Clyde Festivals were born. Radio
Clyde would run a series of events every May in the area
it served under the Banner Clyde XX for the year of the
event. It would provide an umbrella for community events
as well as promoting its own concerts and arts oriented
activities.

I suggested that we should run a free open-air concert
using only local musicians who performed original
material. This would encourage talent on our doorstep
to grow and reach a wider audience. The funding of the
event was possible because commercial radio had in these
days (sadly, no more) an obligation to spend 3% of their
net revenue on live music. This was why Radio Clyde was
able to have its own recording studio and mobile.

At Radio Clyde we had a very good relationship with the Glasgow City Parks Department and provided them with summer roadshows, *Parks Patrol*, with Richard Park – the infamous "Dr Dick". Kelvingrove Park had a great bandstand with a natural amphitheatre and this was chosen for the venue for the first Kelvingrove Free Music Festival.

Kelvingrove Festival Programme

The naysayers said nobody would turn up for unknown bands even it was free but they were wrong. The sun shone, the bandstand was full and an event was born. Sadly, the first Kelvingrove was not recorded but subsequent years were.

The basic principle of original material from local bands was the mainstay throughout the years which the Festival ran, though occasionally we would allow the odd cover song.

Many people still ask what happened to the old Clyde Kelvingrove Festival recordings, and do any of them still exist? Each band did receive a copy of their performance on tape or cassette. Radio Clyde did keep the master tapes over the years but they gradually began to decay. When Radio Clyde was taken over by E-map, a project was set up to take many of the archive recordings and transfer them to digital format before it was too late. The tapes were passed over to River Records who subsequently released many of them. The loft in Clydebank was stripped of all the tapes of name acts and sent for processing. Sadly the Kelvingrove tapes were not included. They would be totally unplayable now and were probably destroyed when E-map or Bauer cleared out most of Radio Clyde's past history.

Matthew C Howe –
Video Director and designer of book front cover

Chapter 9

Braniff Flights 1980 with Andy Collier

Amazing adventures on a trip round the USA on an
airline with the big orange bird.
Andy is a journalist who moved to Glasgow from
England whom I helped with contacts.
He asked me to go with him on a freebie set
of flights to the USA.

I was contacted at Radio Clyde in the late 70s by Andy Collier, a journalist based in England, who was coming to live and work in Glasgow and was looking for contacts. We got on well and he would help me with publicity for the Kelvingrove Festival and Underhand Jones.

He came to me with an idea that we could both make a trip to the USA as journalists with the cost of the flights being paid for by Braniff International Airways. Now at that time I could hardly be called a journalist but I was fascinated by aviation matters. I figured I should go along for a ride and it would be a great break after the 1980 Kelvingrove Festival.

Andy's plan was to go to Dallas and do stories on Braniff and Dallas Fort Worth (DFW) airport then on to New York and Los Angeles before flying home. To get the flights I had to provide a letter outlining what broadcast journalism I would be doing, which thankfully Radio Clyde permitted. We were not permitted to seek freebies in return for airtime so I had to be careful.

So on 27th May we checked in at London Gatwick Airport for the Big Orange Bird as Braniff's 747 was known for the flight from London Gatwick to Dallas Fort Worth. British Airways staff were handling the check-in and there was one critical fact in our booking that we were totally unaware of which we only discovered later in our trip. This was a coding of POSU in our reservation which meant upgrade on space available. So it was economy all the way to DFW. The flight lasted over ten hours but it was under half full so relatively comfortable. On arrival the heat and humidity in Dallas was overpowering with temperatures in excess of 90 degrees Fahrenheit. Throughout the trip we had chosen Holiday Inns as our accommodation of choice. We must have been influenced by Bing Crosby and Fred Astaire from the 1942 movie *Holiday Inn*. We also developed a taste for Pina Colada to cope with the heat.

In Dallas we interviewed Harding L Lawrence, the president of Braniff. He was regarded as a maverick of the aviation industry whose innovations had included painting the aircraft in varying bright colours, high fashion uniforms for the flight attendants and quality in-flight service.

Our second assignment was with the PR for DFW Airport who was a genial host and I found myself consuming a lethal combination of Pina Colada and Guinness which resulted in me back at the Holiday Inn overnight speaking to God on the big white telephone.

The next morning I felt like a couple of Yes albums –

Fragile and *Close to the Edge* as we made our way in our casual travelling clothes to the Braniff check-in counter. There the agent informed us that he could not let us into First Class, as we were improperly dressed. It appeared that we had been marked for positive upgrade on a space available basis for our entire journey. However Braniff had a dress code for upgrades to First Class! A quick visit to the nearest men's room for a change to business attire was all it took but then I wondered why we hadn't received the possibility of an upgrade on the flight out of London.

While Braniff had provided the flights free so we could visit their HQ, they were also keen for us to explore their network so additional free tickets were available to go to New York and Los Angeles.

New York was a major culture shock to me. I had been aware of the "have a nice day" attitude of America delivered in a style that hid its insincerity. New York was right in your face. Everyone seemed so rude. Reality bites! We stayed at the Holiday Inn on 57th Street where nothing seemed to work for us. We even got locked out of our room but an oasis in this sea of rudeness was the security staff that helped us to get back into our room. By this time I had picked up a bit of the New York attitude and at checkout complained about the poor standard of the hotel and got a pleasant surprise. They reduced our bill! Now I understand why New Yorkers complain. Fortunately once I tuned into the New York rhythm on later visits I learned to love the city and its people.

In Los Angeles I had a very brief meeting with a record company executive who politely listened to a demo tape from *Underhand Jones* for about 30 seconds before rejecting it. I suspect that he'd been instructed by their London office to humour me, as Radio Clyde was a very important market for them in the UK. We did the usual tourist things like Disneyland, Venice Beach, and the Queen Mary anchored at Long beach and a drive around Hollywood. We met up with the band *Supertramp* at a Mexican Restaurant in North Hollywood. I had been friends with the band since the release of their breakthrough *Crime of the Century* album and there was a strong Scottish connection through their bass player Dougie Thompson and manager Kenny MacPherson. I picked up a passion for Strawberry Margaritas.

We got the upgrades on all the remaining Braniff Flights except the return to London which was full.

Chapter 10

More Braniff Flights May 1981

Milking the First Class Airpass with Braniff.
Music Producer Clark Sorley from Kilmarnock on a
whirlwind trip around the USA.
It was not surprising that the airline went bust
shortly after this.

On that first trip with Braniff I had absorbed much about the airline, not only about its crazy creative history but what it had planned for the future. They had been trying to take advantage of the Airline Deregulation Act of 1978 which had removed US Government control of airline routes and fares as well as the market entry of new carriers. Prior to that they could only compete on standards of service and discount fares were virtually unheard of.

In 1981, little did they know that in a year's time they would be out of business. Braniff like many legacy airlines became desperate to increase their cash flow and the Braniff Airpass was one device first introduced in April 1979 to do just that.

The Braniff Airpass gave unlimited travel for 30 days on Braniff Routes within the Continental USA. It cost $399 US for Economy Class and $499 for First Class. At that time the US dollar traded at just over two to the British Pound. So for First Class it would be just under £250 that would be worth over £700 accounting for inflation by 2020. The only condition was you had to be travelling from certain destinations outside the USA which of course included the UK. You would receive a book of 16 open coupons and if you used them all up then you just went to the nearest Braniff ticket office to get a replacement!

I figured that this would be a great way to explore the USA and in May 1981 accompanied by my good friend Clark Sorley who was a recording engineer and producer at Radio Clyde with his own successful studio, Sirocco in Kilmarnock. We set out on a crazy USA transcontinental trip using the Braniff Airpass.

We flew on 25th May 1981 from London Gatwick to Dallas on a very cheap discount economy class fare then the First Class Airpass kicked in.

The next day it was from Dallas (DFW) to Brownsville Texas where we had the idea that we should pop across the border into Mexico to the city of Matamoros by walking over the Gateway International Bridge just to say we had been across the border. We wanted to get a Mexican stamp in our passports but were greeted with *"No es possible, Senor"* but with no explanation. Just in case you are inspired yourself to try a trip to this city today, be advised that you are likely to experience the joys of murder, violent crime, robbery, carjacking, kidnapping and extortion for starters!

So back to Brownsville unscathed, we headed to the airport for our flights to DFW and on to Las Vegas for one night then back to DFW for a quick overnight. Then we headed to the West Coast and San Francisco for two nights and Los Angeles for a further two. On June 1st we headed back east to Boston for just one night but got bored there so I figured we should head back to Los Angeles as it had more to offer on the music scene than Boston. Most of this was being done on the spur of the moment. We had three nights in LA before heading to Washington DC for a further two nights staying in Georgetown. My most memorable experience there was a visit to *The Crazy Horse* on "M" Street with its live bands that would play immediately behind the bar at counter level.

On 7th June it was on to the home of Country Music, Nashville (BNA) for a couple of nights. The airport code BNA is derived from its origins as Berry Field, Nashville. The foremost memory I have of that first visit to Nashville was how spaced-out everything was. Not the compact city I had imagined.

9th June it was time to head homeward. Initially, our last First Class sector on the Airpass was to Dallas DFW then back to economy for the home flight to London.

I calculated that we had each eaten and drank more than $500 worth on the Braniff flights alone so it would be fair to say that we could have been a contributing factor to the fact that Braniff ceased operations in May 1982 and filed for bankruptcy!

Chapter 11

Jammy Music Production Library

*Making music for TV, Radio and Movies
at just the right length.
The True Love Orchestra – Wedding Song for
Sarah Ferguson and HRH Prince Andrew.
Producing records with Craig Ferguson in the guise of
Bing Hitler, and noted actors Alan Cumming and
Forbes Masson in their comedy act Victor and Barry.
Movie music success in the USA.*

When Underhand Jones split up I started to look for other artists to work with. I liked the commercial style of *The Imprints* whom I had seen perform at Glasgow's Dial Inn. I signed up two members of the band, Cha Smith and Jim Tollan, as writers for Jammy Music. While working with the band trying to get them a record deal I also saw a market in Production Music also known as Library Music. This is the source of music used in commercials and in background for TV and films whereby producers could get non-exclusive rights to use the music in their productions. As a music publisher we would receive what were known as mechanical royalties for the tracks that were copied on to CDs and DVDs and used in TV, film or radio. These royalties were paid through MCPS – the Mechanical Copyright Protection Society. Additional revenue would come to the publisher in theory for each time the track was played on TV, radio or cinema, played in public or even streamed or downloaded. This would be collected by PRS – the Performing Right Society.

I had spotted a niche market in music tailored for the duration of radio commercials. The shortest length for this kind of tune was 28.5 seconds for technical reasons attached to film commercials on TV at the time. We recorded each instrumental tune into unit lengths of 10, 20, 30, 40, 50 and 60 seconds and distributed these on discs – first vinyl then CD – free to production houses throughout the UK. It was groundbreaking at the time but it became pretty standard.

I also recognised a market in music for movies. I pitched for a TV theme tune to a LA based music house which wanted music for a new TV series based on the *Modesty Blaise* stories. Cha and Jim produced a great demo and while the pitch was unsuccessful it opened the door in Los Angeles for Jammy Music. A deal was set up with the *Fricon Entertainment Company* to handle our material in the USA. We had moderate success with this over the years. Jammy Music's Production Library expanded and was relatively successful but we never landed the big one.

We also did some successful library projects with writers Bill Padley and Grant Mitchell and even brought out a single on BBC Records on 23rd July 1986 to mark the wedding of Sarah Ferguson to HRH Prince Andrew. It was a rather neat arrangement of the two traditional wedding tunes – Wagner's Bridal Chorus and Mendelssohn's Wedding March – played by the *True Love Orchestra* and called *The Wedding Song*. Sad to say BBC Records did not

The Wedding Song Promotional Invite

release it till the day after the wedding but they did create a beautiful cover for the single. Jammy Records also had comedy material. I produced a live solo album with Craig Ferguson in the guise of *Bing Hitler Live at the Tron*. He is now a household name in the States. Then there was *Hear Victor and Barry and Faint* as an EP featuring Forbes Masson and Alan Cumming!

Jammy Records became a vehicle for promoting songs signed to Jammy Music and also for bands who wanted to do their own material and release their own singles. *Jammy But Nice* was a free promotional album mainly for the songs of Underhand Jones.

The reason I had gone with Underhand Jones was initially the simplicity of the songs. They were nice guys and great to work with but I guess on reflection it was the wrong time. There I was trying to push a band of their style at the dawn of the punk revolution! We worked incredibly hard on the songs because that's where the real earning potential is in the music business.

Chapter 12

The Dolphins

*Dangerous fireworks at a midnight open-air concert.
Loyalty to individuals on management contracts
when they go solo.*

I never managed The Dolphins at any point but I took on the role of consultant (unpaid) to advise the boys on their careers. There are so many great memories working with the band. One of the best would be the Kelvingrove Park midnight gig on Midsummer Eve 1983 for not just the crowd but the fireworks. BBC TV News interviewed the band just before the gig and that helped draw the crowds.

I went to Brocks factory in Sanquar to select the "industrial strength" fireworks and studied how to set up a control board to detonate them. We had a moat area in front of the stage and I dug in holes in the ground to place the launch tubes with a safety area surrounding it. During the display one of the launch tubes came unstuck and tottered towards the crowd. I dived over and held the tube in an upright position till it finished discharging, I had no fear as I used to play with Roman Candles as a kid! Very dangerous – don't try this at home. What I didn't know was that there was another fireworks display on the hill above the bandstand. It was Bastille Day at Le Bonne Auberge Restaurant and they had their own celebration, but the crowd thought it was all part of ours!

Stevie Doherty had become the lead singer with Underhand Jones and decided to leave the band. I was still his manager because my contract was with each individual so I worked with him at the early stages of his career with band *Zero Zero*.

This is a basic standard situation in band management contracts whereby each individual is signed up. It covers scenarios where the band personnel changes. It does mean that when a member leaves the band, he can still be under contract. Sometimes the management company will release that person from the contract. In Stevie's case until a new management company came along I was happy to carry out my obligations to look after his interests. We were good friends and I still keep in touch with him today.

I did what I could to help Stevie and *Zero Zero*. There wasn't any formal arrangement but I was still happy to try and help him because I believed in his talent. It might seem a bit naive to say this but a lot of what I did was done on trust. If something had worked out I know I would have had a share of the action.

Chapter 13

USA Trips in Search of Fame

Attempts to get record deals.
Los Angeles attorney hired.
Madam Wong's West is not a brothel!
Foggy Bottom is not something you get
from a strong curry!

I had two trips to the USA trying to pin down record company deals which I was accompanied by the "talent" – one with Cammy Forbes in 1984 and the other with Stevie Doherty in 1987 when he was in *Zero Zero*.

With Cammy then under the brand name of *David Forbes* I set up legal representation in LA with the law offices of Neville L Johnson on Sunset Boulevard. In return for a retainer which we paid, he pushed the bands material to LA based record companies. This was how the music business worked in Tinseltown. We came close, but no cigar. In some ways it was quite depressing. We stayed at the infamous Tropicana Motel (now closed) and dined daily at either Dukes or the appropriately named Fatburger. We spent a lot of time waiting for the phone to ring.

Memories of the trip with Stevie were aided big style by the fact that we both kept a detailed log of the journey which kicked off on Thursday May 28th, 1987. We flew from Prestwick Airport (PIK) with Northwest Airlines to New York JFK. We took an hour to clear immigration, no change there, then a bus to catch the JFK Subway "Express" from Howard Beach which broke down on arrival. A replacement train arrived and we boarded. The train guard whom we assumed had been thrown out of Belsen for cruelty screamed at the passengers to pile their luggage up in the doorways and the doors were then locked to stop muggers joining at intermediate stations. We wondered whatever happened to "have a nice day".

In New York we headed to the World Trade Center to catch the PATH (Port Authority Trans Hudson) Train to Newark City where we planned to catch the bus to the Newark (EWR) Airport. As we headed for the bus stance this old guy hustled us towards his car for a "taxi" ride. As we were about to get in this plain clothes cop in a car with a red light on the roof pulled over and arrested him for no licence, no insurance and no taxi permit! It was an arresting moment for him and a trip on the bus for us. We stayed at the Howard Johnsons at the airport before catching our flight to Los Angeles the next morning with Continental Airlines. As they were running an hour late the Captain declared that drinks would be free. Why does this happen when you are driving on arrival at your destination?

I had booked a "Compact Car" with Alamo which turned out to be well in excess of a Compact being in the luxury class. It was a 7th generation Buick Riviera. It was like a brand new computer game disguised as a car. Everything was computerised with a touch sensitive TV screen on the dash that operated everything from radio, air conditioning, mirrors, windows, cruise control and would indicate any faults or even that everything was OK. When you turned the key on the panel looked like a scene from *War Games*. We reckoned it could do everything except give you a blowjob. Perhaps that was reserved for the up-market model. It took me half an hour to familiarise myself with the controls before I felt OK to drive.

We stayed at the Tropicana on Santa Monica Boulevard with its famous Dukes restaurant next door. I'm not sure if it was anything we did but the hotel was demolished just two months after we stayed there. We did all the usual tourist things in our five days there from Universal Studios to Disneyland, drive through Laurel Canyon, Magic Mountain and visit both Santa Monica Pier and Venice Beach.

We met up with my LA Attorney Neville Johnson and his assistant Don Sylvester who appeared like he would be a stunt double for Don Johnson in *Miami Vice*. We had quite an intense time in LA in their company. This included a trip to a club called Madame Wong's West in Santa Monica. With a name like that it sounded like it should be a brothel, but no. The Madame was Esther Wong who was born in Shanghai in 1917, immigrated to the USA in 1949 at the time of the communist takeover of China. She spent 20 years as a shipping clerk before opening Madame Wong's in Chinatown – a restaurant with a floorshow which tended to be Polynesian dance acts. In 1978 she opened a second venture, Madame Wong's West in Santa Monica. She was persuaded to book punk and rock acts which included The Police, Gun N' Roses and Red Hot Chili Peppers. We ventured upstairs where a 4-piece band called Parallel was playing and they sounded great except – there the sound of keyboards but no keyboard player! They were miming! The microphones were live but only for links between songs. Neville thought they were great but we thought they were cheats.

Monday 1st June was a very full day. We had breakfast at Dukes which was full of music biz types almost like a scene out of *Spinal Tap*. We attended the Showbiz Expo at the downtown LA Convention Center but it was mainly for film and TV though I liked the demo of the Steadicam. I thought it might be good for holding drinks if you've got the shakes. We didn't hang around long and instead headed up to Malibu Beach with a quick pit stop at the Tropicana for beachwear. We managed to park free on the main road just short of Malibu, found a quiet spot beside some rocks and got sunburnt and bored so it was back to the Tropicana for a swim.

That evening we met Don *Miami Vice* Sylvester who picked us up in his car. Most automobiles in the USA are automatic but his was a Volvo with a gearstick. Classy! We met up with Matthew A. M. Powell an English gentleman who was Neville Johnson's business partner and went into Ports at 7205 Santa Monica Boulevard for a few refreshments. We then headed to Le Dome at 8720 Sunset, a very high-class bar and restaurant which sadly closed in 2007. After just one drink (a bit pricey) we decided to move next door to Nicky Blair's where the Scotch was large and plentiful and we had delusions of adequacy, though Matthew wisely stuck to beer.

Thursday 4th June was time to head to the airport and our overnight flight to Washington DC via Newark (EWR). As we had some time to spare we found a pizza place close to Alamo's Depot on Aviation Boulevard which combined pitchers of beer with burnt pizza. Despite that, I enjoyed the establishment as it had large models of aircraft hanging from the ceiling. What intrigued me was a model in Continental Airlines livery of a Boeing 747 but it only had one engine under each wing. As any airline buff knows a 747 has four engines not two. Was this a secret plan by Continental and Boeing for the future? It was a great photo opportunity which I sent to an aviation publication in London much to the annoyance of Continental who didn't like this misrepresentation of their aircraft.

The overnight flight to Newark was on a Continental DC10 which had a "pub" lounge on board. Now I know where Emirates got their idea from.

On arrival at 0630 at Newark (EWR) we had to transfer from the main terminal over to the North Terminal situated on the far side of the runways to catch Continental's New York Air DC9 flight down to Washington DC Airport (DCA). We managed to grab the most disgusting breakfast which consisted of a roll filled with "omelette" which I suspect had been made from a powder that perhaps had been brushed over a chicken at some point. The flight was just 90 minutes and on arrival at National Airport we experienced the joys of a decent integrated transport system organised by the Washington Metropolitan Area Transit Authority. The WMATA had been set up in 1976 to operate the Metro and the Metrobus. It was at that time the second busiest rapid transit system in the USA; the busiest was New York's Subway System. There was a massive contrast between the two systems at that time. The New York System had the dirtiest stations and trains that were not only filthy but covered in graffiti while Washington trains and stations were in pristine condition. While the DC Airport station was on the surface level, the underground stations in the city were magnificent with high ceilings at platform level. It was like something from *2001, A Space Odyssey*.

We walked from the terminal to the station and bought our ticket which cost just 80 cents and would include a bus transfer at our destination station. That station was the delightfully named *Foggy Bottom GWU* (George Washington University). My thoughts of a Foggy Bottom was something you would get from an exceptionally strong curry but in fact the name derives from the late 18th Century when the area was susceptible to fog due to its low lying marshy riverside location. There we caught the Metrobus from K Street to take us along M street then up Wisconsin Avenue to the Holiday Inn in Georgetown.

The visit to Washington DC was more for Radio Station information than Music Business so the next day while Stevie explored Georgetown I headed off to visit NPR – National Public Radio at its HQ on 1111 North Capitol St. NE. While walking round DC can be relatively safe I had been advised that the area between 1st and 19th Streets were strictly no go unless you had a death wish or were desirous of sampling the Emergency Medical Services of the Nation's Capital.

NPR was established on February 26th, 1970 as a privately and public non-profit organisation based in Washington DC established by an Act of Congress in *The Public Broadcasting Act of 1967*. It is funded in the main by corporate subscriptions, donations from public bodies like universities and from their listeners.

After NPR I walked back to the Holiday Inn Georgetown and we headed out for eats to Annie's Paramount Steakhouse. Family owned, it was established in 1948 by

George Katinas and was named after one of George's four sisters, Annie who was the bartender. We ordered *Bull in the Pan* which was their signature dish. Sounded like it was going to be massive but simply put it was steak tips cut from sirloin with a great selection of vegetables.

We then headed to the Crazy Horse on M Street where in one room the band played behind on a stage the bar. The band playing was called *"Gratitude"* with two girls and four guys. They started well with a *Heart* cover then gradually went downhill. We decided not to wait to see if they were saving their best till last. The girl behind the bar having discovered we were from Scotland suggested we go to the other bar where the barman Steve Gillies was from Edinburgh. This resulted in free drinks all night! We left at 2.30am feeling as one does the alcohol induced hunger so we found it mandatory to visit a 24 hour kebab shop for a couple of burgers.

Saturday was a late awakening at 1030am and off to the National Mall to do the round of the Museums including the Smithsonian, the National Museum of American History and the Air & Space Museum. Outstanding for me was Air and Space which was incredibly busy. It was only many years later that I was to discover a better one for aviation was the branch of this one out at Washington Dulles Airport. More on this later. Somewhat tired we headed back to our hotel where we were to meet up with Andrew Manderstam.

Andrew Manderstam was the Washington based correspondent for the UK's London based Independent Radio News (IRN). I had struck up a friendship with him when I was producing part of our overnight Hogmanay (New Year's Eve) show on Radio Clyde. When it was

5 am in Scotland on 1st January, it would be midnight in Washington DC. We would call Andrew at his home in DC and bring in their New Year followed by a review of what had happened over the last 12 months in the USA.

He picked us up and drove us to his house where we met his wife Genevieve. His garden was covered with millions of dead cicadas. They look like insects out of a Hitchcock Horror. They appear like big flying beetles around two inches long and fat. They only appear every seventeen years emerging from the ground casting their shells off and live for only three months when they die after depositing their eggs in trees. These eggs fall off the trees into the ground where they remain incubating for seventeen years before they burrow their way to the surface and start the cycle all over again. This variety of insect only appears on the East Coast of the USA around the Washington Area.

Andrew poured us each a very large whisky but he doesn't drink. Sad to think he misses out on drunken visits to kebab shops and the joys of the hangover. Then all four of us ventured out to a very classy Italian Restaurant DeCarlo's 4822 Yuma Street owned by Lucy de Carlo and had only been opened for around three years. After an outstanding meal, Andrew dropped us off at The Crazy Horse where we tried to catch up with Steve Gillies but he was not around. Perhaps his generosity with the establishment's booze to us had led to a premature curtailment of his career. We tried a couple of other music bars in the area before heading back to home sweet Holiday Inn. We had an early (for us) start on Sunday morning as we were flying to New York Newark (EWR) and then on to Kennedy for our flight back home with Northwest to Prestwick (PIK).

We took a taxi down to Foggy Bottom GWU for $3.50 then the Metro to DCA which was a helluva lot cheaper than a taxi all the way. Our flight to New York arrived at Newark at 1.30pm and as our next one was not scheduled till 7.30pm from Kennedy we explored the World Trade Center. We didn't venture to the top as there were too many screaming kids running around the joint. Then we took subway to Grand Central Station and a walk to Times Square and back. We had decided to go to Kennedy via the Atlantic Avenue Bus Station in Brooklyn where they had a direct bus to JFK. As we passed through Union Square station, we figured the subway itself looked like it had come straight off the set of the 1979 movie *The Warriors* which had been filmed at that location. At the "bus station" which was no more than a hole in the wall we waited for our transport while observing the curious sight of a guy trying to sell assorted meat cleavers to passing motorists. Were they a cut above the rest?

We took a long slow drive on Atlantic Avenue slightly disconcerted to note we were the only white faces on board and mulling over the fact that on our brief visit we never saw Cagney or Lacey. We arrived at Northwest Airlines terminal at JFK at 5pm where we had to stand for an hour at check in. It appeared to us that the Northwest staff were perfectionists in New York aggro to customers as if they are on a permanent bad week. When we eventually got to the gate we discovered our departure time had been pushed back to 10pm from 7.15pm due to a partial strike by the UK Air Traffic Control staff. We went to the bar only to discover it shut at 7.45pm. At that time you could go through security to airside without a ticket. I then went across to the Eastern Airlines terminal where I had membership of the Ionosphere Club but it closed at 8.30pm. We then moved to the Pan Am Worldport where we found a bar that would take plastic and stay open till 10pm. We left the bar at 9.15pm after checking by phone that our flight was still scheduled for a 10.00pm departure and walked back to the Northwest terminal through security and boarded at 9.40pm.

On board they charged $4 for headsets as the delay was not Northwest's fault. The flight was running about 3 hours late and was scheduled to call at Shannon (SNN) in Ireland but at 7.00 am the captain announced we would be going straight to Prestwick! Radio Clyde colleague Alistair Owen met us off the flight and took us back home.

There's an Interesting side note on the total costs of our trip. Our flights were £303 each for PIK-JFK-PIK sectors with Northwest. Continental charged £151 for EWR-LAX – EWR and £59 for EWR-DCA-EWR. The hotels came to $500 US for the two of us and the car hire was $240 + fuel.

In 1987 I did an immense amount of work on behalf of Stevie and *Zero Zero* mainly in the field of legal advice for contracts that were being offered to him at the time. My main interest in Stevie was to sign him up as a songwriter rather than looking after management. I came across a letter in my files that I wrote to Chris Gilbert at Rockmasters Music on 27th May 1987 – they had offered *Zero Zero* a contract.

In this letter I outlined my history of my involvement with Stevie, after he left Underhand Jones in 1979.... Here's an extract from it.

I continued to fulfil my obligations as manager by helping his career including getting him an audition with AC/ DC. Although I kept in touch with Stevie it wasn't until he first formed Zero Zero that I took serious interest in the potential of the new band. Around November last year I noticed the band were cooking well and started to get involved in their promotion, management and business affairs. I made it clear from the start that I had no desires to manage them as my main interest lay in publishing.

I guided them through the minefield of A&R and of bad managers as well as running the publicity machine that led up to the main showcase at Shadows (in Glasgow) where Atlantic saw them in the form of Peter Price and Phil Carson. The organisation included bussing 48 fans from Edinburgh for free, flying Derek Oliver from Kerrang (the rave reviewer) up to see them and in general staging and control of the gig so it couldn't fail.

Chapter 14

Music Scene at Radio Clyde

Creating Stick it in Your Ear!
Hoovered at the Albany Hotel at 3am – T shirts.
Supercharge song story She Moved the Dishes First.
Programme series "Hear Me Talking" –
without the interviewer.
Award winning production The Big Day.

The Music Department at Clyde was incredibly active recording concerts up to five nights a week. The Apollo Theatre in Glasgow was in its heyday. If the concert was on a Friday night we sometimes would record the band and play back excerpts on Steve Jones Boozy Woogie Rock Show at midnight with the band present. After the show we would all retire to the Albany Hotel for drinks with the band and would still be there when the sun came up. Around 3am the cleaner came round the bar area to try and tidy up. Anybody who made it past that hour was entitled to wear the special T-shirt "I was hoovered at 3am at the Albany". This t-shirt was organised by the rep for A&M Records, Stuart Hornall.

In the late 70's I also devised the music magazine programme *"Stick It In Your Ear"*. This was at the time quite cutting edge whereby we would interview artists then edit out as much as possible, especially the interviewer, and mix it with key snippets of music. It was great fun to produce with Brian Ford as the presenter. We chose a magic piece of instrumental music from Tom Scott & the L.A. Express called *"Good Evening Mr and Mrs America and all the Ships at Sea"* which just happened to be on A&M Records. That creative rep for A&M, Stuart Hornall, organised pin badges for the show to be given to all artists who appeared on it.

We could be quite cruel at times but usually to our own. When the lead singer and saxophonist Albie Donnelly from the band *Supercharge* came in for the show, Richard Park was to do the recorded interview. Unfortunately Richard was not in the mood for Albie's humour. A pity because one of my favourite tracks from the band (not the then current single) was *"She Moved the Dishes First"*. This was based on the claim that his girlfriend was really posh and when she had a piss in the sink she moved the dishes first! Richard opened the interview by asking Albie about the new single to which Albie replied, *"I don't want to talk about the single. I want to talk about a cure for my baldness!"* Richard stopped the interview saying if you can't be serious we won't continue. So they started all over again. On *Stick it in Your Ear* we played both versions!

I had a philosophy at Radio Clyde that in music interviews it was far more important to hear what the guest had to say than the interviewer. Some interviewers become so overcome with the exuberance of their own verbosity that the guest has to ask, "What was the question again?". I devised a programme format called *"Hear Me Talking"* in which the interviewer (often me) would be edited out and the just the guest's responses used with appropriate extracts from their songs to illustrate the point they were making. It was very pacy and as it had no presenter other than the star we were able to share the shows with other commercial radio stations. One example was an interview I did with Nick Lowe who had signed to Warner Brothers in 1978. They liked it so much that their head of promotion made 55 copies of it and sent it around the world for radio stations to use.

In 1990, Glasgow was the European Capital of Culture. An event took place that was one of the highlights of my career at Radio Clyde – *The Big Day*. This featured four live stages throughout the city. We covered it live with stereo feeds from each of the stages into our studio HQ in Clydebank and four live roving units with a reporter and production assistant. I drew on the crews from our Superscoreboard sports team to resource the event and approached it in the style of live golf tournament.

Every song was recorded from each stage and itemised so it could be played back instantly. Bands included Hue and Cry, Wet Wet Wet, Love and Money, and Big Country. We were honoured with a Silver Medal at the International Radio Festival of New York for our coverage.

Chapter 15

Million Miles on Northwest

How to win as a frequent flyer.
Thanks to Saddam Hussein for my Million Mile status.
Sick Northwest aircraft gives me
First Class Singapore Airlines experience.
Finding the way to San Jose.
Etiquette in Thailand.

By January 1984 my interest in aviation was growing stronger. At that point my flights had been limited to a few holiday charters, my El Al to Israel in 1969, First Class with Pan AM in 1975, then in 1980 and 1981 the joys of Braniff (Chapters 9 and 10).

On 30th January 1981 I made my first trip with Northwest Airlines (NWA) which operated a service between Glasgow Prestwick Airport (PIK) and either Boston (BOS) or New York Kennedy (JFK). At that time there were no Frequent Flyer Schemes as we know them today in the aviation world but a few months later that was all to change.

Rolfe Schellenburger was the Manager of Marketing Planning for American Airlines in 1980 and had been tasked by his bosses to come up with a way of rewarding the loyalty of individual travellers who flew major amounts of trips with a free trip to Hawaii as thanks for their business. He headed up a team that devised and implemented the *AAvantage Travel Rewards Program* on May 1st, 1981. Their expectations were modest for the scheme reckoning if they were lucky they might achieve 50,000 members by the end of the year. Their forecast was so far out that it made a builder's "estimate" feel accurate. Over a million customers signed up to the scheme by the end of that year. Naturally, rival airlines all came up with their own schemes to compete. Ten years later there were in excess of 28 million members on the various North American airline schemes with on average each customer holding cards for 3.5 of the schemes. While Hawaii was purely a token destination the idea was that any destination on their network would be available. Now these profoundly frequent flyers probably had their fares paid by the companies they worked for so it was really a bonus for the individuals.

Joe Brancatelli the editor of *Frequent Flyer* magazine at that time said that they were the most effective marketing programs the airlines had ever created. While implementing the scheme would cost money for administration and to a certain limited extent in free flights, the airline was saving money on advertising as they now had a more effective way of reaching their customers through the membership mailing lists.

At that time American Airlines were also leaders in inventory management systems. They could predict with remarkable accuracy based on the history of the route and key events from conventions to holidays how many seats they expected to sell in First and Economy classes on any route. From that they could put into their system "Super Saver" fares which had real restrictive terms like advance purchase of say 28 days, no change and no refund rules. This would steer them clear of the business traveller who required flexibility but would help them fill up seats that would otherwise be empty. While a flight may be divided into First Class and Economy Class, the inventory management system would sub divide these into what is referred to as "fare buckets". They were able to allocate, where prudent, a bucket for free frequent flyer tickets. Revenue management is an incredibly complex subject but in my studies of the subject I have been greatly aided in the past from *"Flying Off Course: The Economics of International Airlines"* by Rigas Doganis.

It was not until April 15th, 1988 that I started flying with any degree of regularity with Northwest Airlines usually connected with promoting material for Jammy Music. I was on a trip to Tampa, Florida, for a holiday and on to Los Angeles for Jammy Music. At check-in they suggested I should join their WorldPerks Frequent Flyer Scheme and earn rewards for all the miles I flew with Northwest and their partners. I didn't really consider myself as a "frequent flyer" but just in case I flew with this airline again I should sign up. Little did I realise this was the first step to becoming a mileage junkie addicted to gaining miles and status. I found myself doing what they called mileage runs towards the end of each year to either keep my status or move up a tier in the awards scheme.

I started racking up the miles with Northwest and by the end of 1989 I achieved Gold Elite status which had benefits like free upgrades to First Class on domestic flights on a space available basis and a percentage of Bonus Miles added to my account for each flight. From 1988 till the start of the Gulf War in August 1990 I made eleven transatlantic trips with a total of 92 flights and around 138,000 flown miles.

I had a great relationship with Northwest Airlines and their Country Manager Bob Buntin who was based in their Glasgow office in Renfield Street. He had recommended that I should use Blantyre based Glen Travel for all my bookings as they were consolidators for Northwest. A consolidator is a travel agency or tour operator who will have a contract with an airline to help them sell seats as part of a package deal. It would be unfair of me to deny that the fact I worked for Radio Clyde helped me in the preferential treatment I received from NWA but it paid off big style. And as my Frequent Flyer Status in WorldPerks climbed I suppose there was some justification on their part.

It is utterly selfish for me to say how grateful I am to the Iraqi idiot dictator Saddam Hussein but his actions leading to the Gulf War had a massive effect on my mileage status. Demand for Transatlantic flights dropped massively and Northwest introduced bonus miles of double and sometimes triple for the actual flown miles to stimulate traffic.

Between October 1990 and April 1991, I made four transatlantic trips with a total of 30 flights and around 56,000 flown miles so my WorldPerks Account was overflowing once the bonus miles were added.

On 12th of June 1992 I was booked to go to New York on behalf of Radio Clyde to attend The International Radio Festival and pick up some awards including one of the top Grand Awards. I was booked on the direct flight NW35 from Glasgow to Boston and connecting on to New York's La Guardia arriving at 5pm in time for the Awards

Ceremony that evening. As was my practice I checked on the internet very early that morning to make sure all was running to schedule. I discovered to my horror that the inbound was running four hours late and as a result the delay to the outbound would mean I would miss the Awards show!

I rushed straight to the airport and spoke to Northwest Airlines Customer Service Manager, George Cobb, to see if anything could be done. Using a process called a FIM – Flight Interruption Manifest – he rebooked me on a BA flight to London and then on to an American Airlines flight direct to New York's JFK Airport. While my Northwest flight had been in Economy it turned out that American put me in Business Class as apparently their Economy Cabin was sold out! Joy of joys, I ended up arriving in New York two hours earlier than I would on my original Northwest flights!

At the Awards Ceremony I had picked up a rather large silver bowl which was the Grand Award for Radio Clyde. The next day I was scheduled to fly from New York Newark to Anchorage, Alaska with Northwest on one of my crazy "it would be cool to go there for a day" trips. My WorldPerks Status meant I was entitled to space available upgrades on any domestic flights within the contiguous states of the USA. Now that's a big word they use but it simply meant this perk was not available to Hawaii or Alaska as it is not joined to any other state. Pretending to be geographically challenged I asked at check-in if there was any space available in First Class. The agent initially said it was not possible but then went into a back office to check with a colleague. He returned with a smile on his face and a First Class Boarding Card in his hand.

I was travelling light on this trip so the silver bowl had to go with my carry-on bag. Not surprisingly it set off the alarm at the security checkpoint appearing on their screens as some sort of dodgy device. Anchorage was stunning, I had a full day there in the clear air and a delightful 60 degree Fahrenheit temperature so I hired a bicycle to explore singing the Michelle Shocked hit song, Anchorage.

Northwest also had a great character in their UK management team in the form of Ian Yates. He was their Operations Manager but also a specialist in handling dangerous goods. I always wondered if I came into that category because he, I hope, jokingly said if he found me on any flight he was on he would have me offloaded. In fact the opposite happened when he found me in Economy on a transatlantic flight we were sharing, he had me moved into Business Class! He would be sent by Northwest to their airports in Asia to teach their cargo handling staff how to deal with the transportation of dangerous goods. His main concern was Asian cultures whereby to save face when being taught they would not question anything they heard if they didn't understand it.

There were many tales of his management manner but my favourite was when he had to handle a technical diversion into Glasgow for a flight from the USA that was bound for Frankfurt, Germany. The problem could be fixed by their Glasgow ground engineer but while repairs were being carried out, the flight deck crew were in danger of running out of duty hours. The Captain had a degree of discretion in this but to encourage this decision Mr Yates removed the steps to the aircraft so the crew could not get off!

On my frequent transatlantic trips I got to know many of the crews, so when it came to Thanksgiving on November

22nd, 1990 I decided to throw a small party at my flat for the crew who were going to be away from home on their Glasgow layover over that Thursday night. The winter schedule was operating so they did not have a flight back home till Saturday so alcohol and food was provided and they could watch the NFL Thanksgiving Game on my TV.

My WorldPerks Miles were stacking up faster than a toilet roll hoarder during the 2020 Covid-19 Pandemic, so I figured it was time to spend them in some degree of luxury especially as the mileage rewards for travel from the USA to Asia for First Class Travel seemed very enticing.

I fancied a trip to Thailand and decided I would buy an Economy Class return ticket from Glasgow to Los Angeles (LAX) then use my miles for a free First Class ticket from LAX via Honolulu and Tokyo Narita to Bangkok's Dom Muang airport and back. I didn't know much about Thailand apart from the girls being beautiful and the food amazing so I asked my Travel Agency, Glen Travel, for some advice. It's a family business out in Blantyre and while David Glen Senior was the owner his three sons, David Jnr, Alan and Douglas also worked in the agency.

Young David had recently been out to Thailand so I sought his advice on where to go and in particular how to strike up a relationship with Thai Bar Girls. To do this I took him out to lunch in Blantyre but he found when it came to the girls he found it slightly difficult. He didn't know me that well however I was able to establish some basic etiquette in how to engage with these girls. Things like how you have to pay a "bar fine" if you want the girl to go with you and how much you should reward her when it was time to part company. Put quite simply prostitution has been illegal in Thailand since 1960 so payment was never discussed in advance. He also recommended Pattaya as the best place to visit.

So on September 15th 1992 I ventured out for my first of what was to be many Thailand trips. It was a strange feeling on the way from Tokyo to Bangkok as we flew over Vietnam seeing all the place names on the moving map display of cities burnt in my memory from the Vietnam War, which had finished 27 years earlier, like Hanoi, Da Nang and Saigon.

Over the next 12 years I made 12 trips to Pattaya in all with Northwest in First Class using miles except for one with KLM. Some of the flight attendants with Northwest looked old enough to have served with the Wright brothers at Kittyhawk! This was not an issue as I preferred to have someone looking after me that had experience and could cope in an emergency rather than one who was just pretty. My flights to Thailand were to continue right up to 2019 but with Emirates in the driving seat.

My view of Northwest was just an average airline but they did look after their most frequent flyers extremely well. The best example of this happened in July 1997 when I'd made my usual Frequent Flyer Free First Class Ticket from the USA to Bangkok.

On the way home I checked in at Dom Muang Airport at 3 am for my 6 am departure to Tokyo NRT and onwards to San Francisco. The flight was called as normal and we went to the bus gate at 5.30 am for departure. At 6 am there was no sign of boarding for this flight which looked pretty full. Then the gate agent announced, "Please, First Class and Business Class come forward. Everyone else please stay in your seat."

Once we came forward to the podium the Agent addressed us in a whisper. "Plane sick. Plane not go. We rebook you on other airlines". I thought that as I was on a FREE Frequent Flyer Ticket they wouldn't put me on another airline but wait till the first available Northwest flight. I knew their schedule pretty well and I determined that if they got the aircraft fixed swiftly I could make it to Tokyo in time to catch another flight to Honolulu. Then I would go on to San Francisco arriving around 12 hours later than planned. Failing that it would be the next day's departure which would have been fine by me, as I really did not want to fly on a "sick" plane. I was to be stunningly surprised.

"Mr John", the agent addressed me in a way I loved, "We have you rebooked in First Class on Singapore Airlines. You will fly to Singapore then on to San Francisco with a stop in Hong Kong. You will arrive at your destination two hours later than scheduled with us. Very sorry for inconvenience."

Sorry? Inconvenience? I was ecstatic! Singapore was the most awarded airline in the world with outstanding service so I was ready to be impressed. The flight down to Singapore on a Boeing 737 in Business Class was OK. The onwards service Singapore to Hong Kong on a Boeing 747 in First Class then crew change for the last leg to San Francisco was stunning. The service and food were immaculate but what really impressed me was one of the simplest things to do yet so many airlines miss out. It's called profiling. For each customer they note what preferences they have then pass the information on to the next crew. So as we approached San Francisco the flight attendant approached me and asked "Mr John, would you like anything else before we land?". I asked for a cup of tea and she said without hesitation "With two sugar and milk as you had when you left Singapore?". She had studied my profile provided by the previous crew and memorised it so she knew her customer's preferences. It was so simple, costing nothing but very effective.

While I thought Singapore Airlines (SQ) were outstanding, I was very mindful of the fact that it was due to Northwest Airlines taking care of their top end customers that had given me the experience. I calculated that a one-way First Class ticket from Bangkok to Singapore with SQ would cost in the region of $10,000 US. When I got home I took the time to write to Northwest saying while my Singapore Airlines experience was amazing, the reason I would be keeping my business with Northwest is because they really look after their top tier customers when things go wrong. Boy, do I know how to crawl!

In March 1996 I received from Northwest Airlines my Million Miles Certificate and my gold baggage tag which I was extremely proud of thinking that I was one in a million (some say I was won in a raffle). My pride took a fall when shortly after that I was storing my bag in the overhead locker on a flight and noticed that the bag next to it had a two million miler tag on it!

March 1998 NWA forced all UK based WorldPerks Members to switch to KLM's Flying Dutchman programme. This would mean I lose my Gold Double Miles Bonus, Unlimited Free Domestic First Class upgrades and devalued my benefits to 25% of what they were worth. I wrote to John H Dasburg, President and CEO of Northwest Airlines. Dasburg quit Northwest in February 2001 to head up Burger King for a different kind of whopper.

To understand my next move with WorldPerks to keep my membership alive I have to digress at this point. Back in 1989 in the world of football the Under-16 world championship was being held in Scotland. At Radio Clyde I received a call from a Bob Higgins who was temporarily based in Scottish Television's HQ in Glasgow but was working for a California based company who had the contract to provide worldwide television coverage of the tournament. He had a request for technical assistance in providing radio commentary, not in his normal remit, for one of the games for a radio station in Ghana. STV had recommended he contact me and I was happy to provide assistance. After this Bob and I became friends and he let me know about another business in which he was involved. That was the Studio Center on South First Street in San Jose, California. He suggested I should drop by on my next trip which I did. There I met up with Mathew C Howe who was a musician and video producer. This was the start of a long friendship. I signed him up as a writer for Jammy Music and though nothing really came of that there were many other interlinked activities in my life that followed.

I certainly did *Know the Way to San Jose* which is a fascinating city, the third largest by population in California. It is multi-cultural and this is shown in the signs on the transit systems which are displayed in English, Spanish and Vietnamese! This was as a result of post Vietnam War immigration.

I took Matt over to Scotland a couple of times using my WorldPerks Miles in Business Class to video the Kelvingrove Festival. As a result of this friendship I was able to use Matt's home address in the City of Campbell in California as my mailing address for WorldPerks when they forced European based customers to switch to KLM's Flying Dutchman programme and on each visit I would pick up my mail from Northwest.

My last Northwest flight was in October 2002 at which time I cleared out most of my WorldPerks Miles with a First Class round trip from California to Thailand. I then switched my remaining miles over to KLM's inferior Flying Dutchman programme and changed my flying loyalty over to Continental's One Pass which is covered in the next Chapter. All my experiences with Northwest had been pretty good and the contacts I had made were more than helpful in making my radio documentary *Tales from Kai Tak* in Chapter 19.

Kai Tak Airport Hong Kong

Chapter 16

Doing the Continental

How to emerge from bankruptcy in the USA.
Hawaiian Goddess Madame Pele.
Doing the tango in Buenos Aires.

This may be Chapter 16 but I'm going start this one with the potential to confuse you by talking about "Chapter 11". In the UK in 1983 when a company declared bankruptcy, administrators were appointed, any remaining assets would be sold off to pay creditors and the company was wound up. In the USA under Chapter 11 of their bankruptcy laws, in simplified terms, a company could present a restructuring plan to preserve a slimmed down operation. This would protect the company from creditors while allowing time to reorganise. Invariably there would staff layoffs and reduced salaries for those returning to work for the restructured company.

Continental were in deep financial difficulty by 1983 mainly as a result of the effects of airline deregulation in 1978. In the years that followed, Continental's losses were over half a billion dollars, 50% of that was in 1983. Chairman and Chief Executive Frank Lorenzo tried to get the unions to accept salary and working conditions changes but they refused so major surgery was required by filing for Chapter 11 bankruptcy. On September 24th, 1983 Continental ceased all domestic operations. The following Tuesday they resumed a much limited service. They cut staff from 12,000 to 4,000 and they reduced the cities served from 78 to just 25. The unions for the flight attendants and the pilots called a long and bitter strike which was not settled till 1985. So how did they keep flying? It was a combination of non-union staff and those union members who decided to cross the picket lines.

I was fascinated by how the bankruptcy laws worked in the USA and chose the Continental bankruptcy as a subject for a documentary on Radio Clyde in 1985 called *"Doing the Continental"*. I approached Continental in the UK for assistance and they were very obliging by flying me to Houston and Washington DC. I was surprised at how open they were because in Houston they allowed me to wander round the crew areas unescorted by any PR person and talk to employees. There were some heartbreaking personal stories but the underlying theme was – better to have a job than nothing at all. One of the union's tactics was to claim that Continental's flights were unsafe because their members were on strike. I visited the Federal Aviation Administration HQ in Washington DC where they showed me how they had increased their inspections of all Continental maintenance facilities and allowed me to take copies of some of their reports. The union claim was unfounded.

During my visit to Washington DC I also called in to the Smithsonian National Air and Space Museum and in particular to meet up with a fascinating Englishman, Ronald Edward George (R.E.G) Davies, Curator of Air

Transport. He ended up holding the post for a remarkable 30 years. He gave me access to the museum archives on the history of Continental. I was delighted to be able to meet with him as he was the author of *Continental Airlines The First Fifty Years 1934-1984.* He was born in London on July 3rd, 1921. In 1939 he signed up as a Territorial Volunteer in the British Army taking part in the Normandy Landings in 1944 driving a machine gun carrier. After the war he had a variety of aviation related jobs including the government's Ministry of Civil Aviation, British European Airways, The Bristol Aeroplane Company and de Havilland. He emigrated to the USA in 1968 to work for Douglas Aircraft in market research before "retiring" from that post and moving to the Smithsonian in Washington DC.

In studying the archives I came across the history of "Air Mike" and the story of how Continental set up Air Micronesia to provide essential air services in the North Pacific between Honolulu and Guam which was known as the *"Island Hopper"* covering Majuro, Kwajalein, Kosrae, Pohnpei and Chuuk (Truk). This triggered in me a "must try this" as the 16 hour flight could be fun. The results including my plans for a 10 part TV series are described in Chapter 20.

I took some internal trips with Continental in May 1987 flying from New York to Los Angeles and Washington DC. At that point I had signed up to the "One Pass" frequent flyer scheme on my principle that you never know when you'll fly that airline again but it's worth joining just in case. Little did I know that I was on the road to becoming a "Million Miler" with Continental and subsequently, when they merged with United, it transferred to "Mileage Plus". As part of the Star Alliance I achieved "Lifetime

Gold" status which I would retain as long as I did at least one flight a year. Benefits included lounge access on any international flights, free upgrades and increased bonus miles.

My next experience of Continental was in June 1987 when the airline in partnership with the Hawaiian Visitors Bureau organised a "Press Trip" to these Pacific islands. A "Press Trip" has the purpose of enabling journalists to write or broadcast favourable stories about the destinations or services involved. To ensure the warmth of the participants, copious amounts of food and alcohol would be offered. The danger of such fine hospitality is that you find the memories of the outing can disappear in alcoholic oblivion. We flew from London Gatwick non-stop to Denver where we had a remarkably speedy clearance of Customs and Immigration then on to Honolulu. Andy Dougan one of the News Editors at Radio Clyde gave me some basic training on Hawaiian language and customs like, they have the same word for "hello" and "goodbye" – aloha! Also essential would be "Mahalo" for thank you. Then there was the history of the islands and its first ruler King Kamehameha who reigned from 1782 to 1819. If you think that name is a mouthful then try his full name – "Kalani Pal'ea Wohi o Kalakini Krealii'ikui Kamehameha o 'Iolani i Kaiwikapu kau'i Ka Liholiho Kunulakea"- a lot of words that simply mean "the quiet one". His sex life was anything but quiet having had between 21 and 30 wives according to historians.

Anything but quiet is also the active volcano Kilauea, known locally as "Madame Pele" on the Big Island. People get confused about the Hawaiian Islands of which there are eight main ones. The island of Hawaii itself is known as "the Big Island" partly because it is the biggest but also to avoid confusion with the island of Oahu where you'll find Honolulu the State Capital, Waikiki Beach and Pearl Harbour.

The most memorable part of this trip was about the flight attendant on a small inter-island flight from Honolulu to Maui who noticed that some passengers (our journalist party) who were first time inter-island flyers were showing concern about the steam pouring through the air vents as the plane climbed out of Honolulu. He took the PA microphone and said, "Do not be alarmed by the steam coming through the air conditioning units. This is perfectly normal in this kind of aircraft in tropical climates. Were anything to go seriously wrong, I would be the first to let you know as I left the aircraft!"

It wasn't until 1998 when Continental started a regular non-stop service from Glasgow to New York Newark that I started to rack up my "One Pass" miles and by the end of 2002 I had racked up 43 flights with a total of 75,000 miles.

With Continental I was constantly searching for new places to visit and in 2006 I made two trips to South America via the USA. In January I visited Buenos Aires in Argentina and took a round trip Air France flight to Santiago in Chile where to my delight I was upgraded. I had some concerns about my arrival in Argentina even though it had been 23 years since the end of the Falklands (Las Malvinas) War so with some trepidation I took a taxi from the Aeropuerto (EZE) to downtown Buenos Aires. The taxi driver asked me *Ingles?* To which I replied *Escoces!* and a big smile came on his face. He then said "Jackie Stewart" the Scottish racing driver who won the Argentina Formula-1 Grand Prix in 1972! We became the best of friends.

I fell in love with Buenos Aires where grilled meat (parrillas) was stunning. Vegetarians please look away! Portions were massive and the steaks were scrumptious. At one restaurant the steak I ordered reminded me of the episode of *The Simpsons* first aired in 1999 (Season 10 episode 17) where Homer takes part in a meat eating challenge against trucker Red Barclay. While mine wasn't quite up to the 16 lbs Meat Mountain that Homer devoured it certainly felt massive. It took two hours to cook and a further hour to devour. I also loved the tango shows which would feature a meal and a live orchestra and dancers. I always thought that the male participant of the partnership in the tango has to be very trusting of the female as part of the moves involve her kicking her leg towards her partner's crotch.

The return to Argentina was in June 2006 and after that the miles rolled on with Continental and in 2007 I added Lima in Peru to my next South American Destination. Although I had some limited understanding of Spanish – *Hablo un poco d'Espanol* I had great difficulty in understanding public transport system in the city. Try this mix of privately owned big buses, medium sized micros and small vans called combis. While this convoluted network connects most of the city's main streets the full routes and timetables of the micros remain a mystery. Buses and Micros can be waved down at any point on the main road. I did a lot of walking round the city trying to figure out how it worked. The locals knew what they were doing but I feared causing an international incident by attempting to board one myself.

Chapter 17

Climax in Pattaya

The Thai word "porn" is not what you may think.
The horizontal leisure centre.
Website for the Climax Rock Band.

That first trip to Thailand described in Chapter 15 had generated a love for Pattaya and it was not just the attractiveness of the girls, or the excitement of making sure you hadn't been chatting up a ladyboy! This did happen till the Irish Bar Manager put me right. There was a vast range of food and amazing clothing that the Thai tailors could create at rock bottom prices. For my second trip in 1993 David my travel agent had recommended that I switched hotels from the delightful but remote Thanaporn which was about 3km from the centre of town at the bottom of Cliff Road in the direction of Jomtien Beach to one more centrally located. My choices to reach the Thanaporn were walking up a steep hill past the Big Buddha Temple in the sweltering heat, taking a taxi (expensive) or a motorbike taxi (dangerous).

A point of clarification is required here. A Thai name that contains the Thai word "*porn*" simply means blessing. For Westerners this Thai word often leads to confusion, misunderstanding and dirty laughter. If you must know the word in Thai for the English "porn" is *Sox Lamk* but not recommended you use it as Thai pronunciation is very difficult.

The hotel in Pattaya that David recommended was in the heart of the action in Walking Street in the southern end of the city. Walking Street is so called because it is closed to all traffic in the evening. It is the home to girlie bars, live music, restaurants and nightclubs. That hotel was the *Diamond Beach* located in *Soi Diamond* in Walking Street. What was unusual about his recommendation was that the hotel did not pay any commission to Travel Agents but he would still be making something on my flight bookings. This was true service, looking at the bigger picture and one of the reasons that Glen Travel kept my business for a long time. Now to the hotel itself. It was certainly not a diamond nor anywhere near the beach but at £15 per room per night with breakfast and good security with a rooftop pool it suited me. Understanding their market they had a sign saying "no charge for visitor girl in your room". Security required that any "visitor girl" had to hand over her ID card to them. If they had no ID card you would have to sign an indemnity form to take responsibility for her. The local English language newspaper the weekly *Pattaya Mail* had a delightful turn of phrase in describing the hotel as a "horizontal leisure centre"!

By the end of the decade I had made eleven trips to Pattaya. For the third trip I had decided to put myself into the mood by going out for a meal at a top class Thai Restaurant in Glasgow – the Thai Fountain at Charing Cross. Much to my surprise all the staff were Hong Kong Chinese except one. Her name was Pawina and I happened to mention to her that I was going out to Thailand in a couple of weeks to Pattaya. A big smile came on her face. Well, Thais always seem to smile but this was special. Her sister lived in Pattaya!

She stunned me (apart from the smile) by saying "I give you some medicines and money to take to her when you go". Here she was trusting a complete stranger with this mission! I gave her a conditional acceptance but I insisted that anything she gave me could be opened and inspected by security at the airports. I was too familiar with the standard security question of carrying something on behalf of another person. I returned to the restaurant just before I set off on my trip and she gave me her sister's address in Pattaya in Soi Yensabai along with some money and the "medicines" which proved to be harmless.

When I arrived in Pattaya I got hold of what I thought was a decent city map. Soi Yensabai twisted its way through the back roads of the city for about two miles but no house numbers were shown on it. I set out on my mission to find her sister's house. I located Soi Yensabai but could not fathom out the numbering system for the houses. They seemed to jump all over the place. I asked some locals showing the address but they couldn't help. Back at the Diamond Beach I asked reception if they could help. They recommended I go along to the Post Office, as they would be certain to know where it was. An extremely helpful assistant was able to show me on the map where I could find her house. Apparently houses are given numbers in the order in which they are built! So house number one will not be next door to number two or three unless it was constructed at the same time!

I arrived at the designated address which opened up into a courtyard with about 16 single storey dwellings in a rectangular block. I found the long lost sister who unfortunately could not speak English but with the help of a neighbour was able to convey her gratitude and ask me to stay till her husband Chaub came home. I did and we struck up a long lasting friendship. On each subsequent trip I would go to their house for a meal and then take them out a couple of nights later to one of my favourite restaurants, the Ruen Thai, which we nicknamed *the dangerous restaurant* on No 2 Road. The reason for this title of "dangerous" was fun. As well as having a fine traditional Thai cabaret floorshow, the open-air venue featured waiters rushing through the premises with flaming hot food dishes. One slip and the flaming food would go flying. I was surprised how direct Thais could be in conversation. How much do you earn? It was best to be honest.

In Walking Street there are many live music venues which mainly feature Thai rock and blues bands doing songs in English. The one I settled on was the Climax Bar which featured the Climax Rock Band which did remarkable covers of artists like Deep Purple, Jimi Hendrix, Led Zeppelin, Queen and Pink Floyd. Their lead guitarist is Peak NokZaak whose outstanding skills on interpretations of rock classics wowed the audience. After a couple of visits I asked the owner of the venue "Champ" if I could make a website for the band and the venue and so Climaxpattaya.com was born. As well as photos and videos of the band I thought it would be useful to provide a guide to Pattaya for visitors. Included in this were guides on changing money, (surprisingly best to do this on arrival at the airport), transport and how to behave!

John with Climax Band Pattaya

Respect is a keynote to Thai society. Do not say anything to offend the Royal Family. Try and learn a few words in Thai, they'll love you for it. Do not get involved in drugs in any way. The penalties are severe and life in a Thai prison is not a good way to extend a holiday.

While the band sang in English, they were very limited in conversation. The website expanded and followed the band as they changed venues when Champ sold the Climax Bar in 2007. The band wandered around a few venues before Irishman Steve Young gave them a new home further along Walking Street at Utopia. Their complete history was on the website and the last I heard they were in residence at the Toi Bar on No 2 Road just opposite the Big C Shopping Centre. Around 2016 I created a fan Facebook page for them and stopped updating the website.

Understanding relationships with Thai bar girls is important. Many come from Northern Thailand to seek money to support their families back home. You pay a "bar fine" to take the girl away with you. Traditionally you do not discuss money for her company, as this would be tantamount to prostitution which is illegal. This is rather a moot point. When it is time to part company you reward your girl with a cash payment. If you really like the girl you may chose to stay with her for a long time but you would reward her each day. The danger of going into any long term relationship is you could find yourself supporting her family and she will start making demands on you for more money to send back home. For those who go the whole way and marry the girl you'll find she has a lot of relatives!

Apart from the food and the girls, there was also clothing which was incredibly cheap. I had several Thai tailors during my visits but finally settled on Louis Tailors on Beach Road just before Walking Street. I designed my own trousers which were with black cloth, front loading vertical square pockets and a side utility pocket for my phone. I never have understood why traditional tailored trousers have side pockets which are so easy to pick. Mine were tailored to fit, usually ready within 3 days and I would order several at a time. Cost for each was around £20.

Chapter 18

Claymores in Europe

Why American Football has more hanging about than in a clothing warehouse.

Prior to 1995 my understanding of American Football (NFL – National Football League) was zilch! It struck me that an awful lot of people spent an inordinate amount of time busy doing nothing. There was more hanging about than in a clothing warehouse.

It was a massive moneymaker in the USA in part due to TV rights. For most of the rest of the world the word football meant soccer. Europe was and still is a hotbed for soccer but due to the presence of American Forces, there was an interest in American Football NFL style.

In the USA, the TV audience could watch live games from September through to February. In order to fill in the gap for live games the NFL in partnership with Fox TV set up The World League of American Football which went on to become NFL Europe. The title "World League" was a bit of an exaggeration as the teams featured only came from Europe but with most players from North America who were sent by their parent clubs to see how they would perform. The teams also had a number of "National" players who were not attached to any NFL USA franchise but usually were local or from outside the USA.

In 1995 the World League was reorganised to consist of a six club all European based group with $40 million backing from the NFL and FOX TV. The clubs were Frankfurt Galaxy, Rhein Fire, Barcelona Dragons, Amsterdam Admirals, London Monarchs and The Scottish Claymores. The Claymores looked like being the toughest sell as Scotland had no history of American Football influences; even London had NFL pre-season show games. As well as coverage on Fox in the USA, in the UK we were treated to Sky Sports (live), Channel 4 and Scottish Television for highlights.

Curiosity may have killed the cat but not being of feline origin I felt no life-threatening vibes when I took the opportunity to attend the first Claymores home game at Murrayfield Stadium in Edinburgh on Sunday April 9th against the Rhein Fire. Radio Clyde was part sponsor of the Claymores so I managed to pick up a free ticket to the game in true Scottish spirit.

Up until that point my knowledge of the game was very limited. I knew they played four 15-minute quarters so why did the match last up to three hours? All will be revealed. The official programme was helpful in understanding some of the basic rules of the game. Why were there so many players on each side? A soccer team would have eleven + substitutes but an NFL team would consist of several sets of players and substitutes plus one set for when the team is on "offense" (in possession of the ball on the attack), one set for "defense" and one set known as "special teams" to handle kick offs, punts and field goals. I hope I'm not losing you so here is a very simplified form of the game that I perceived from my virgin outing.

Each team when on the field is allowed four attempts to move the ball forward by at least 10 yards referred to as "downs" – First Down, Second Down, Third Down and Fourth Down. If at the end of the Third Down they have failed to achieve at least ten yards from the point they started the series of downs, they would normally kick the ball as far down the field as possible at which point the opposing team would take over possession. Sometimes when there is just a very short distance to go to get a new set of downs, the team will elect to go for it on Fourth. This can be quite dangerous if they fail to achieve the distance the opposing team takes over possession at that point.

Points are scored by a "touchdown" which is achieved either by passing the ball to a receiver in the "End Zone" or carrying the ball over the goal line. Unlike in rugby the ball is not require to touch the ground to score but simply break the plane of the goal line while in controlled possession of the player. I could never understand why they call it a touchdown when the ball doesn't touch down on the ground. Once they score a touchdown they can add an extra point by kicking the ball through the uprights of the goalpost which is known as "the point after" of try for a two-point conversion by throwing a pass to a receiver who takes it in the end zone. Purists will argue there is a lot more to it but I like to try and keep it simple.

So why is the match so long? It's all stopwatch timing. The clock starts on each play when the ball is snapped into play and stops again when the ball goes out of bounds or on referee's whistle. Each team has 3 breaks known as "Time Out" in each half when the can stop the game for consultation with the coaching staff on the sidelines. These normally last 30" but can be much longer if the game is being televised live to allow for commercials.

Now here's a very useful tip if you are at a game that's live on TV and are desperate to go to the toilet but don't want to miss any of the action. Try and spot one person on the side of the field wearing headphones and bright orange long sleeved gloves. This will be the TV floor manager whose job it is to indicate to the officials on the field that TV is taking a commercial break which can be several minutes long. That person will walk onto the field with his arms crossed to indicate TV commercial break and you know you'll have your own few minutes comfort break.

Each team would have coaching staff consisting at minimum of a Head Coach, Offensive Coach, Defensive Coach and Special Teams Coach. Each play in the game was normally pre-planned from their playbook which would consist of hundreds of plays to cover different situations. Communication with the Quarterback would be by radio for the offense and by hand signals for the defense. Prior to each game the coaches would study film of their opponents to look for weaknesses. The best way to follow it would be as a massive game of chess with live pieces on the board.

Although the Claymores lost the game, my interest was sufficiently aroused to want more. So when I returned to Radio Clyde the next day I asked our Sports Department if anyone had official accreditation to cover the Claymores games. Not surprisingly since they were so soccer orientated nobody had picked up that mantle and so they let me go ahead and be the accredited reporter.

I have to say this for the NFL, they really looked after the press. We had pre-match hospitality, a seat in the press box with a supply of all the statistics as the game progressed, and access to the post game press conference with further hospitality.

I bought a copy of the Official Rules of the NFL 1995 Edition to help me understand the game. Surprisingly there were only 18 rules in the book. This will be easy – not! Each rule was divided into sections and had Articles attached to them to cover every possible situation. If you really must know them then get your own copy from the NFL.

My enthusiasm for the game led me to following the Claymores home and away in the 10 years of their existence. Radio Clyde had no budget for covering NFL games so I paid my own fare and accommodation for flights to Frankfurt, Dusseldorf, Amsterdam, Barcelona and later Berlin where the Berlin Thunder joined NFL Europe replacing the London Monarchs.

I became great friends with the coaching staff especially Head Coach Jim Criner who had taken over the top job just days before their first game in 1995 when their designated Head Coach Lary Kuharich was fired. Jim Criner is famed for taking the Claymores "from worst to first" which he proved when they won the World Bowl in Murrayfield in 1996. I continued following the Claymores right up till their demise in 2004 when the NFL decided to pull the franchise. It struck me as rather odd that the NFL had failed miserably to capitalise on 40,000 fans that had attended the World Bowl at Murrayfield in their second year of operation.

I did take advantage of my press accreditation to catch a couple of games in the USA, one in Atlanta for the Falcons and the other in Tennessee for the Titans. I was very impressed with the organisation behind both.

Chapter 19

Crazy Radio Clyde Career

*How TV shutdown at 1030 pm made Radio Clyde
an outstanding success.
The Great Crossini escapologist on the radio.
Princess Margaret meets the Wombles and
Uncle Bulgaria is arrested.
Winning a Rover Sterling car.
Tales from Kai Tak.
Mallan in Manhattan.
The Assistant DA from Orange County,
California becomes Radio Clyde presenter.*

In December 1973 Britain was in crisis. How unusual you may think? Little irritants like high inflation, miners' industrial action and world oil prices had forced the Government at the end of the year to introduce a three-day working week. Most power stations were coal fired so to reduce consumption and preserve fuel stocks, commercial consumption of electricity was reduced to just three days a week. Perhaps not the best time to launch a new business especially a commercial radio station. TV was made to shut down at 1030pm every evening.

When Radio Clyde launched on 31st December 1973 despite the doom and gloom in the country we were full of optimism. It wasn't till our first set of audience figures came out in early 1974 did we realise how well placed that optimism was. Our biggest benefit turned out to be television or lack thereof! At 1030pm after TV closedown, people searched for an alternative on their radios and found Radio Clyde. Imaginative programming gave listeners in Glasgow and West Central Scotland a new source of locally produced late night entertainment. A different presenter each night on the 1030pm till 1.00am slot brought names like Frank Skerret, Don Cumming, Colin MacDonald, Arthur Montford and Iain Anderson on to entertain on the West of Scotland's wireless. The audience would tune in and when they went to bed their radios were on 261 metres on the medium wave – Radio Clyde's broadcast frequency on AM – with the catch-line *Radio Clyde 261 Altogether Now* on all the station jingles. In the morning when they woke up they discovered a new kind of local breakfast show and stayed tuned to discover Dave Marshall!

As the crises continued through the winter we were called into a staff meeting whereby Managing Director Jimmy Gordon laid down just how difficult things were but he hoped we would manage to soldier on without any redundancies. Then with an air of optimism he asked for a representative from each department to join in a discussion about a profit sharing scheme!

Much of my time in these early days was spent resourcing our programmes. The key was local content and I stressed to all involved how important it was to give out full name and street addresses whether it was from a letter or a phone-in caller so the audience would recognise all things local to them in people and places. I really detest the style that later crept into broadcasting whereby they would only give out the first name and area of the caller. It could be anybody. I suspect this may have been brought in by lawyers! OK, there would be times where the identity of the caller had to be protected but these were rare.

While I would seldom be on air, there were in these early days a few occasions when I could be heard. Taking the radio station to the streets in the form of outside broadcasts was part of my remit. We had a couple of Radio Cars and a mobile caravan. In the summer when our sports programme Superscoreboard took a break, we mounted a 4-hour Saturday show which covered live events all around our area trying to visit as many locations as possible. Bellahouston Park was the location for a "spectacular" involving a variety of circus style performing acts. One of them featured an escapologist called The Great Crossini who would be secured in a straight jacket then hung upside down 100ft in the air from the jib of a crane and escape! I was to interview him live as he made his escape so they made a cradle for me and attached it to the jib so I could reach out and interview him as he did his amazing escape. No Health & Safety in these days! All went well except for the organisers deciding it would be a great idea for my commentary to be relayed to the crowd at the event through the PA system. The result was horrendous feedback because my microphone picked up the PA sound and produced a loud howl.

While that event was planned, another was certainly not by me. Journalists in Commercial Radio belonged to the NUJ – National Union of Journalists. At one point in the 70s they were in dispute with the management at

Independent Radio News (IRN) in London, the company that supplied news to commercial stations throughout the UK. As we worked on the principle of the world through West of Scotland eyes, we would rewrite their news copy and use their audio cuts but never their live bulletins.

Rather than going on strike in this dispute, they would call a mandatory "chapel" meeting at which point their services would not be available to the management. The term "chapel" did not mean that they all traipsed down to the nearest church for some religious ceremony; it was just the term they used for their union branch. Although the dispute was London orientated they instructed all "chapels" in commercial radio throughout the UK to hold meetings at the same time.

That afternoon both Jimmy Gordon and Alex Dickson, Head of News, were out the building when the "Father of the Chapel" Stuart Millar called on me. Now the term *Father* just meant the leader of the branch except on this occasion he also happened to look after religious affairs at the station. Confused? He came to me at around 3.30pm and said "You're the most senior member of staff here, so I have to inform you that we are calling a mandatory meeting of all journalists and we will be unavailable from 3.30pm till 6.00pm." He then told me that they did not really want to be involved in something that was just a London dispute so they had prepared the 4pm news bulletin and the complete 5pm Newsdesk Magazine which lasted half an hour and all we had to do was present it.

I was non-union at that time. In fact my only union membership had been with British Rail when I was a member of the Transport and Salaried Staffs Association. I had attended just one branch meeting at which only five people had turned up to discuss some critical proposal. It was all comrade this and comrade that, but I only felt that I wasn't among friends, only apathy.

So I read the 4pm bulletin which went fine but the Newsdesk magazine at 5pm required the services of a technical operator (TO). They had decided to go into their own "meeting" and be unavailable for the programme. I advised them that if nobody appeared for the show I would be forced to take disciplinary action against them. I actually hadn't a clue what I would do so I was somewhat relieved that 5 minutes before showtime a TO appeared for duty in the studio.

I would also earn some supplementary income by voicing commercials. Our sales team came up with the novel idea that I should do a few of these live from a local furniture store to promote their new sale (I reckon it must be written in law somewhere that furniture stores must always have a sale on). This would have been fine except the script had the opening line of "I'm speaking to your from inside a wardrobe at Carrick Furniture House" so to ensure it sounded right I actually went into the wardrobe with the door partially closed to voice the commercial!

During the 70s we had some wild outside broadcasts. Every Sunday during the summer Richard Park would host *Parks Patrol* from some of Glasgow's fine city parks featuring Doctor Dick's Dancing Dollies and visiting guest stars. On one show we had the full line up of The Jackson 5 featuring a rather young Michael Jackson!

On another planned roadshow the weather had turned nasty so we abandoned the OB location and retreated to the studio complete with the dancers to add atmosphere. Interestingly enough I helped one of the dancers join Equity the actors union on the basis of her contracts to perform on the roadshows. Her name was Christine MacInnes and she went on to have a successful career on stage as a dancer. We hit it off rather well and to put it mildly she was very attractive with a big future in front of her. I took her out for a holiday to the West Coast of the USA visiting the likes of Las Vegas and San Francisco. We flew Business Class with Northwest and I had my first experience of real luxury when we stayed in a rather large suite at the MGM Grand. It had two bathrooms one of which was bigger than my apartment back in Glasgow. We had a hire car and took turns at driving. Sad to say by the end of the trip we had started to drift apart and on the flight home we chose seats apart from each other. While we split, we still remained friends.

One roadshow we did in Buchanan Street in Glasgow City Centre hosted by Richard Park featured a guest appearance by *The Wombles* which attracted massive publicity due to the fact that Princess Margaret was also on a visit to the city and when she spotted them her Royal Highness stopped for a chat. This was a great photo opportunity. One side note which did not receive the same attention was the fact that Womble Uncle Bulgaria (well, the actor who was in the costume) had to appear the following morning at Glasgow Sherriff Court on a charge of being drunk and disorderly. It seemed that after his Royal encounter he went off to sample the delights of the pubs in the city.

Warner Brothers had a big star in Ralph McTell with his *Streets of London* hit but they were concerned that he was quite shy. Their head of promotion Bill "Foxy" Fowler talking to Andy Park came up with the idea that Ralph should come to Radio Clyde and stand in for Steve Jones on the mid-morning show while he had a week's holiday. I looked after Ralph by producing the show and working the desk. As the week progressed his shyness disappeared and the audience took to him.

As he was a London Eastender I decided to take him out to Glasgow's East End for a couple of drinks at lunchtime after the show. Now at that time the East End of Glasgow was not the most pleasant of surroundings but I was interested in the adventure. Not such a good idea. As we entered the first bar we were met by the glare of the regulars who did not seem to like strangers on their turf. A few started singing what would be regarded today as sectarian songs just to let us know what religion you should be to survive on the premises. I figured that our continued presence was likely to lead to our demise and so we beat a hasty retreat back to the city centre.

Here are a few more tales of experiences during these fun days.

We were recording a Barbara Dickson concert at the Apollo. In the recording truck Mobile Two was an engineer who had a tendency for non PC observations on the talent. We had a monitor screen of the stage so we could see the artistes while recording. Also in the truck at the back was her husband Oliver Cookson but our man was not aware of his presence when he remarked of Barbara – "I'd like to give her one!" Fortunately Oliver never heard him and we discretely made our errant engineer aware of his presence.

The story goes that on our routine checks with hospitals one responded with a story about an outpatient who had been treated for the removal of a vibrator in their rectum. The patient could well have been one of our DJs so we would sometimes ask him what's the buzz?

Frank Skerret hosted a twice weekly show called "When Music Was Music". Humorous and cantankerous, he would read out listeners' letters complete without editing them. His humour was borderline with lines like "the one good thing about being a widow is at least you know where your husband is at night!" Listeners would sign off their letters with "regards to you and Maureen." Maureen or "the Maureen" as we called her in the office was not his wife but his partner on roadshows which mirrored his radio shows. One night a gang of us attended one of his shows and incurred his displeasure when we held up scorecards after each joke.

One of our fine Music Producers was Bob McDowall who had an expression he frequently used – "fuckin' frightening". Gordon Giltrap of *"Heartsong"* fame was in our music studio with me recording an interview when Bob walked in unaware who my guest was. He mentioned something about Gordon Fuckin' Giltrap as he came in. So I took the opportunity of introducing them to each other!

Supertramp and Chris de Burgh had come from their Glasgow concert straight on to the rock show with Steve Jones. They all had brought acoustic instruments with them and played live covers of songs except for Chris who did his own stuff. I was in the control room mixing the show while Steve Jones was in the studio. Timing is so important in radio so when we were approaching the news scheduled for 2am, Chris started playing a song beautifully back timed to the news. Now a little sidetracking on this event. I had invited a young lady to the studio whose house I had visited to deliver a prize the previous Sunday. The prize was a hunk of beef which her mother had won live on air on Richard Park's Sunday Lunchtime Show on which you could win a Roast from the Host with the Most. I delivered it straight after the show. Mother had a rather attractive daughter who was interested in what went on at Radio Clyde so I invited her along to the Friday night Boozie Woogie Rock Show. I have to say it was quite difficult concentrating on doing the mix while this young lady insisted on rubbing her crotch against my leg. So after the show she spent the night at my flat. Somehow the word went round the station that not only could you win the roast but also a shag from the producer.

In 1980, Dougie Donnelly held his stag night on a Friday at his flat in the West End. Naturally I was there but had to present the Saturday Morning Breakfast Show at 6am. On this occasion my passion for presenting radio was overtaken by my consumption of Bacardi rum but as a precaution I had written on the palm of my hand "if found please return to Radio Clyde before 6am Saturday". I staggered into Radio Clyde at 5am and asked Charlie our security guard to wake me at ten to six. I then went into the cloakroom cupboard and crashed out on the floor for 45 minutes. Charlie woke me up at the appointed time at which point I went to the toilet and stuck my head under the cold tap to freshen up. I picked up all the records for my show which I had fortunately prepared the night before. I was conscious that I was pretty pissed so I decided to keep talking to the minimum. I made it to 8am and went home to sleep. Later that afternoon I returned to the studio to check the log tape of the show as I could not remember anything about it. Fortunately my autopilot mode had produced no disasters.

On a visit to San Francisco I visited a sex shop – all in the interests of research you understand – and I had purchased a blow-up sheep. I brought it back to Radio Clyde and somehow got the reputation of being a sheep shagger. DJ Mark Page took an interest in Flossie the sheep as she became known and bought it from me so he could use it at roadshows. Well, that was his story!

In the early days at Radio Clyde we had a lovely gay newsroom assistant called Bobby Boylan. Some mornings he would appear in the newsroom somewhat bruised and battered having tried to chat up the wrong "trade". He also liked going out dressed up in a wig and women's clothes till one time he tried to board a bus using his pass with his (male) photo on it. The driver then threw him off as the photo on the pass didn't match the image in front of him!

Julie McGarvey was a Production Assistant at Radio Clyde. She was working the phones on one of our consumer programmes when she had a rather tedious caller on air. She hit the talkback button on the phone system which she thought was going to just the presenter and she said "get off the line you silly old bat" Unfortunately it went out on air! I'm glad to say it did not do her career any harm as she ended up running her own very successful PR company.

In the 70s it was the time of "the troubles" in Northern Ireland. As a security precaution all incoming mail was scanned by a metal detector. A small package addressed to Sydney Devine with an Irish postmark had set off the alarm. We called the police to assist. A wise old sergeant took the package outside to a piece of waste ground. He then informed us that we can either call the bomb squad or just dispose of it with the old fashioned method. We hid behind a wall and threw bricks at it until it burst open. Inside was... a pair of cufflinks!

Our nightly news special at 5.30pm was a 30 minute show with headlines, features and live interviews. It was presented by our news team from Studio A with its own mixing desk and presentation area as well as from the separate news booth which had a glass partition giving line of sight between the two areas. A technical operator (TO) would sit at the control desk playing in all the audio cartridges and mixing the live microphones. On the control desk there was a tiny toggle switch that made one channel operate either on the news booth or in the main studio. In theory the news producer would bring in all the audio to the TO at least 5 minutes before the show started. On this occasion Dave Murricane was on the desk and Craig Samet was the producer. At 5.30 Dave ran the news jingle as Craig wandered into the studio late with all the audio. There was no time to line anything up but newsreader Bob King in the booth waved across to Dave to indicate that he would start the show with the headlines. Dave hit what he thought was the toggle switch and gave Bob the cue to start. He then took his own headphones off and shouted at Craig. "For fucks sake, you fucking newsmen are never on time for this show. Get a fucking grip." Then to his horror he noticed the meter on the desk seemed to be responding to his own profanities. It had all gone out on air. He quickly sorted things out and in the production office I awaited the calls of complaint. Nothing! Fortunately for Dave the microphone which had gone live was somewhat distant from him so the swearing was only in the background. The next day I did receive an inquiry from a convent in Motherwell asking what had gone wrong. I explained that a technical area had accidentally gone live and apologised for any inconvenience. They seem very happy with my explanation.

Radio Clyde was full of characters and not just among the DJs. In our newsroom was George Montgomery who had a remarkable talent for doing impressions. One evening on Tiger Tim Steven's show George had the audience convinced when Tim invited them to phone in and talk to "Dean Martin", "Jimmy Stewart", "Frank Sinatra" and "John Wayne". George was with Clyde till 1979 when an incredible opportunity came his way to go to live and work in Hong Kong as an Assignment Editor with RTHK which was the official government run station. His voice talents came in useful when he took a sideline of dubbing Cantonese Kung Fu movies into English. One time when doing a Jackie Chan movie he was messing around during the changing of reels and as a joke he gave Jackie's character a Humphrey Bogart voice! The trick backfired when Jackie asked him to do the rest of the movie in that voice! George escaped by telling Jackie that he could do it for one or two scenes but not for a whole two-hour movie. George had an amazing government flat on Hong Kong Island at Jardine's Lookout which gave a view across the harbour to Kowloon and you could watch the planes take off and land at Kai Tak Airport. I was lucky to go and stay with him several times including being present for the "handover" of Hong Kong back to China on 1st July 1997. He and his family were pretty worried then that the next day the Chinese army would move in and round up all the expatriates and shoot them! It didn't happen.

Our Outside Broadcasts took us overseas mainly to the USA for some memorable events. For these overseas operations we only required a live two-way link back to the studio in the UK. The music and commercials in the show were inserted back in Glasgow and all we had to do was provide the live links plus any pre-recorded material.

We had a time difference of five hours between the East Coast of America and the UK so when we decided to take George Bowie's breakfast show (6 am to 9 am) out to New York in June 2000 it meant that it would be 1 am to 4 am which was not a bad idea for the "City That Never Sleeps". We picked Times Square to be the ideal location. We received technical assistance from ABC Radio whose studios were conveniently located in Times Square and set up on the pavement (sidewalk) outside their premises. Now this was convenient for more than technical reasons as you would normally need a City Permit to do this on a public sidewalk but ABC actually owned the area outside their studios so no permit was required. Our crew was just three; George and his producer Sara Procter and me. All looked great till ten minutes before we were due to start a works crew arrived from Con Edison the major power company with the intention of drilling through the night right in front of our location! I had some pleading words with the foreman who to my delight said they could switch to another project and come back later! Afterwards when I got home I wrote to Con Edison to tell them their crew were a credit to New York City. They probably got fired for their kindness!

We also partnered with the Walt Disney Organisation to present live shows from their Walt Disney World theme parks in Florida with Mike Riddoch as the host. Disney were top notch in their facilities and organisation but they did this for broadcasting organisations from around the world so you would find several mini open air studios set up all round the parks. A "minder" was attached to our crew to ensure that guests were not annoyed by our presence and we respected Disney ethics. Our minder was actually from England and was most un-Disney like when off duty. In fact he was great fun. We learned from him that there were several "cast members" in Mickey Mouse costume in the park but great care was taken to ensure that two could never be seen in the same place at the same time. Facial hair was not permitted for any cast members unless it was part of a costume. Smoking was not permitted so our minder would take his ID badge off and go behind a building for a cigarette!

While Mike Riddoch's shows were live we also did a series of five "as live" programmes at Disney properties coast to coast with Scottish entertainer Alastair MacDonald as host. We covered Walt Disney World's three Florida parks on the East Coast plus on the West Coast Disneyland in Anaheim and the Queen Mary in Long Beach California which at that time was owned by Disney. Over a two-week period we recorded all the links for the shows, fed them back to the UK where they were played out "as live".

For two weeks we trekked coast-to-coast. Well, it was hardly a trek travelling by plane from Florida to California and with a hire car at our destinations. Alastair was a very patriotic Scot and it was an annoyance to him (and to me) the way in which folk in the USA use the term England when they meant the United Kingdom. Just to clarify, the United Kingdom at that time meant England, Scotland, Wales, Northern Ireland and Wales along with the Channel Islands and the Isle of Man. So using the term England to a Scot was akin to calling someone from Canada "American" or from New Zealand "Australian". Unfortunately by the time we reached the Queen Mary in Long Beach, Alastair had gone native. In interviewing the Captain of the Queen Mary, that fine liner, which incidentally was built in

Clydebank, Scotland, he used the phrase "back home in England". Ouch!

This trip was at the time of the first Gulf War and when we reached Los Angeles hostilities in the Middle East had just broken out with a major offensive by the coalition forces. The scene on Hollywood Boulevard was unreal. Many shops were deserted except those that had radios or TVs where crowds gathered round to hear the latest new live from the Gulf. Piped music was replaced with relays of all news radio stations. It was a scene akin to a country at war, which indeed it was.

Back now to a simple domestic fight in the UK. I made a day trip flight to London 13th November 1988 with Air UK that was to have a massive benefit for future travels. Air UK had just won the right to serve the Glasgow to London Gatwick route against stiff competition. They branded the route "Sterling Service" and to promote it they ran a rather tasty contest to win a brand new Rover Sterling Car worth over £19,000. To enter, all you had to do was estimate the total number of passengers that Air UK would carry on their network over a set period of time. I had fun on the trip calculating the total number of seats available then estimating the average load factor. I sent my entry off and forgot about it. A couple of months later a letter dropped through my door to say I had won as my entry was the closest to the actual total! Wow!

A presentation ceremony was arranged at Glasgow Airport where the car was parked on the apron. I had no real need for a second car as I already had a company vehicle so I sold it to my partner in Jammy Music, Andrew Harvey. I used the money to fund my future flights and I'm happy to say that many of them were with Air UK or their partners like KLM/Northwest.

In October 1991, slipping on my Travel Editor's hat, I was invited by British Airways to experience Concorde! I was flown on 25th October from Glasgow to New York with a 3-night stopover. On 28th October I boarded BA 002 from JFK departing 1215 and scheduled to arrive at London Heathrow at 2100. The flight time was just 3 hours 15 minutes, compared to 8 hours on non-supersonic aircraft. Inside the cabin it felt quite small with just 92 seats in a two by two configuration. You could feel the thrust of the engines on take-off but when we went through the sound barrier there was no sensation at all. The only way you knew was an indication in the cabin of the speed at which the aircraft was travelling. While food on board was outstanding, I considered the cost of the flight against the cost of a normal First Class ticket. A one-way ticket for Concorde was in the range of £4,350 while a First Class ticket was just £1440 for non-supersonic flights. The clientele for Concorde tended to be high-powered business executives to whom time was precious or showbiz stars who liked to show off! While it was a once in lifetime experience, if I was a regular on that route and had the money, I would have stuck to First Class on the normal aircraft with all its associated comforts.

Overseas travel became part of my lifestyle for work and play and my enthusiasm for aviation related matters was probably best illustrated when I decided late in 1997 to make a radio documentary on the closure of Hong Kong's Kai Tak airport and transfer to the new facility at Chep Lap Kok on Lantau Island.

I already had two aviation related documentaries under my belt; *Doing the Continental* in 1985 (see Chapter 16) and *BY300A* which took a flight deck trip from Glasgow to Orlando on a twin jet single aisle Boeing 757 to show listeners the behind the scenes operation of the regular charter flight operated by Britannia Airways.

For the Hong Kong project one minor stumbling block was to be justifying the programme on Radio Clyde without a Scottish "Nose" but that was to resolve itself in quite a stunning manner. A Scottish "Nose" is a journalistic term for giving an international story a weighted local basis sometimes out of proportion to the original story. A great example of this was the claim that an Aberdeen newspaper reported the sinking of the Titanic with the headline "Aberdeen Man Drowns at Sea". In fact it wasn't quite like that but never let the facts stand in the way of a good myth.

It was around nine months in the making and would involve several trips to the USA and Hong Kong including a couple of landings where I had the privilege of being present on the flight deck.

As was the form in these days if you had a programme idea for a documentary you had to do it in your own time and while the facilities of the radio station were at your disposal luxuries like travel expenses were a strict no-no!

Kai Tak was probably the most challenging airport in the world for pilots of big jets to fly into. At most large airports in the world, aircraft use an instrument landing system (ILS) to assist in landing, especially in bad weather. This worked by sending out a radio beam from the end of the runway giving the exact alignment and recommended glide slope for aircraft to use to achieve a perfect landing. On board the aircraft the ILS technology would "capture" the beam at a predetermined altitude and lock on to it thus assisting the pilot with the approach and landing. It could be used at many airports for an automatic landing. This would be impossible at Kai Tak because of the surrounding terrain.

To explain this you have to understand the geography of the area. Kai Tak Airport was located on the Kowloon side of Hong Kong and it had a single runway 13/31. Runways are numbered by compass directions so if you were heading 130 degrees it would be Runway 13 and if it was going the opposite way, 310 degrees then that's runway 31. If as in some massive airports like Atlanta Georgia USA you have two or three parallel runways then you would add to the number L for left C for centre and R for right.

Aircraft must land and take off into the wind to produce maximum airflow past the wings at minimum speeds. If you had a tailwind you would have to land or take off at much higher speeds. The prevailing wind at Kai Tak was normally blowing around a heading of 310 degrees so runway 13 would be in use most of the time. Now this would be fine for an ILS system if it wasn't for a pesky little mountain over 3000ft high getting in the way. So what aircraft had to do was approach the airport at an angle that was 47 degrees off the glideslope until they reached the extended centreline of the runway at an altitude of just 600 feet and then make a sharp 47-degree right turn onto the glideslope, wheels down and land. You felt that you could grab the washing hanging on the lines out the windows of the high-rise buildings at the edge of the airport.

The weather was frequently lousy with heavy rain and strong winds making a real challenge to keeping a large aircraft in the air. To assist the pilots a checkerboard was installed on a small hill just outside the airport to mark the point at which they should make their right turn. Added to this was an Instrument Guidance System (IGS) which was similar to the ILS but did not lead to the runway, only the turning point. Airlines required special training for their flight deck crews before they were allowed to operate into Kai Tak.

It was a pretty challenging job for the pilots The TV series *Most Extreme Airports* on the History Channel rated it No.6 in the ten most difficult at the time. For pilots in these days of automation this was real flying.

The origins of the airport go right back to 1912 when two businessmen Ho Kai and Au Tak formed the Kai Tak Investment Company to reclaim land in Kowloon for a development which actually failed so the Government bought the land. In 1924 it became the home to the Abbott School of Aviation and several flying clubs plus the RAF (Royal Air Force) made use of it. During the Japanese Occupation of Hong Kong in World War 2 proper concrete runways were built. The runway received several extensions till in 1974 it was 11,130 ft. That year the IGS – Instrument Guidance System – came into operation.

My plan was to talk to pilots, the airport operator and air traffic controllers about their experiences at this icon of aviation before it closed. Using various aviation forums on the internet I sought out potential contributors. Journalists are as popular in the aviation community as a fart in an elevator. They were regarded as vile pests who only sought sensationalism. Example; a simple standard safety procedure called a "go around" when the pilot has to cancel his approach due to possible conflicts would be a screaming headline of a dangerous near miss by ignorant journalism. It was a case not of pilot error but of journalist error.

I could have done what most forum contributors did and hide my identity. No way! I needed to be upfront so I used my real name and stated my mission. I was instantly flamed, but the forum moderators stepped in to my defence. Fortunately by that point I had a track record of producing informed journalism on aviation matters and the flames were extinguished. My quest struck a chord with many pilots so I set out to try and interview a cross section of experienced aviators many of whom were based in the USA.

The response was wonderful as I heard back from active and retired pilots from around the world, many in the USA, who had some great stories to tell but I struck gold when David West, a training captain and weather expert with Hong Kong based Cathay Pacific got in touch. It was to be the Scottish connection that my bosses at Radio Clyde required for any resulting programme to be aired. David was born in Scotland and had taken his first flying lessons at Glasgow Airport. He had a wealth of information to provide so much so that he ended up being the thread that held the show together and gave me access to valuable contacts in Hong Kong. I wanted to experience from the flight deck a landing at Kai Tak. He arranged a special permit for me to join him on a round trip from Hong Kong down to Denpassar (DPS), Bali in Indonesia.

This was an amazing trip not without incidents. On the flight down to Bali we received information that the DPS airport was temporarily shut due to an aircraft stuck on the runway so I watched the meticulous planning he carried out for possible diversions. Fortunately the airport reopened and we landed on time. The return trip started with an issue of weight as the flight was totally full. When they checked the load sheet which accounts for the total weight of everything on board the aircraft David discovered we were 10 kilos overweight. He took a simple solution and instructed the flight attendants to offload a couple of cases of soft drinks and that would bring the weight down to within legal limits.

As we neared Hong Kong the weather became really nasty with thunderstorms, hailstones and gusting winds. He let the First Officer fly the aircraft while he could concentrate on the weather radar which gave pretty ominous readings of the flight path ahead. He would manoeuvre the flight around the thunderstorms and occasionally brushed with hailstones which he quickly got out of saying "the company don't like it when we return the aircraft with dents!" He was in constant touch with Air Traffic Control (ATC) to advise the need to change altitude or direction due to the severe weather. It was a pretty bumpy ride and everyone had to be firmly strapped in. David was so calm throughout. Fifteen minutes before we were due to land he buzzed through on the intercom to the lead flight attendant to ask "Any chance of a cup of tea?" It was a perfect landing.

I had an excellent friend in Hong Kong in the form of ex Radio Clyde newsman George Montgomery and stayed with him while I did my research. He gave me some good local contacts including the General Manager at Kai Tak – an Englishman called Tony Norman.

I approached various airlines which served the airport for assistance and several were extremely obliging, in particular British Airways, Northwest Airlines and of course Cathay Pacific. British Airways were extremely helpful and arranged for me to fly on their nonstop London to Hong Kong flight just to get the landing and from the perspective of the flight deck. They had a minor issue over the fact that any time a journalist was on a project like this, they had to be accompanied by a member of their PR team but they had nobody available! However as I had such a good working relationship with them they decided I could go unescorted on the trip and boy did they look after me. I flew in First Class in both directions on a Boeing 747-400 and managed to capture some excellent audio on the landing from Captain Nick Bristow which I used to close the resulting programme. This was typical of the time spent on achieving around a minute's airtime.

Northwest Airlines didn't give me a flight deck trip but went one better by setting up a visit to their NATCO training facility in Minneapolis with time on their Boeing 747 simulator to demonstrate how they trained pilots to fly into Kai Tak and how they would cope with emergencies. Training Captains Tim Olson and Jim Hancock made it feel like the real thing.

The response I had received from the Professional Pilot's Rumour Network (PPRUNE) on the internet had been overwhelming. I had a mix of pilots who flew or had flown passenger, freighter or military aircraft over a long period from the early days to present. As many of them were based around the Minneapolis St Paul area of Minnesota I set up a meeting with around five of them to get their stories. They included Dick Duxbury a retired 747 captain with Northwest and former Chief Accident Investigator, Chip Crosby a 747 Captain with United Parcels Service (UPS), and Tom Erickson Northwest 747 Captain.

I made three other stateside visits to track down more contributors. Manny Puerta a retired Check Pilot with UPS lived near Reno, Nevada and I had to make two separate transatlantic trips to reach him. The first was in January and I had flown to San Francisco with the intention of driving to Reno. This was a big mistake. To reach Reno by car you have to drive through the Donner Pass – elevation 7056 ft on Interstate 80. Heavy snow would cause closures and snow chains were required at certain times on this route. As I drove on I80 through Truckee, the snow started to fall quite heavily and eventually it was a whiteout. I decided to abandon my trip and return to San Francisco and home to the UK. I called my pilot friend who totally understood that safety always comes first. When back in the UK I rearranged the trip for a couple of months later and also I would fly into Reno and meet with him at a local hotel which worked fine.

To complete the picture I needed access to the operations at Kai Tak including ground handling and especially Air Traffic Control (ATC). This took a lot of time to arrange as the airport was under the control of the Hong Kong Government. Eventually the Airport General Manager Tony Norman gave the go ahead and did an outstanding job in arranging access to the control tower permitting me to interview controllers and record the ATC transmissions.

I reckon I had spent over 1000 hours of production time on the project and it was finally aired on Radio Clyde on the week of the airport's closure. To ensure accuracy and because I had been given privileged access to the operational side of things I gave final approval of all content that had involved such access like flight deck operations to those involved. This saved me from one particular embarrassment when for the introduction to the programme I had written a line saying "flying through thunderstorms" and David West was able to correct me to say "fly round thunderstorms" as aircraft never intentionally fly through them!

Peter Mallan

One of the productions of which I am most proud in my career at Radio Clyde was in 1995 with *Mallan in Manhattan*. Scots entertainer Peter Mallan had a regular Friday night show *Mallan till Midnight* which had a mix of Scottish music and classic opera. Peter had a fascinating history. As a youngster born in Glasgow in 1934 and brought up the Gorbals area he was always singing. His talent was recognised by the renowned Scottish Tenor Canon Sydney MacEwan who tutored him. He had a variety of jobs on leaving school at 15 before joining the Glasgow Fire Service at the age of 21. As music was his first love, in his early 30s he set off to London where he gained a degree from the Royal Academy of Music. His singing career and recording career took off. He was the first artist to record the Scottish song written by Jimmy Copeland *"These are My Mountains"*. In 1967 Peter went across to New York where he lived and worked for a year or so. He'd crossed the Atlantic on the *Queen Mary* in a force 12 storm. While in New York he sang at Carnegie Hall and the Waldorf Astoria, and worked as the Almoner for the St Andrews Society. We decided to take him back to Manhattan and we revisited 32 different locations that had featured in his life in NYC. At some locations Peter would burst into an appropriate song. He sang on top of the Empire State Building, The World Trade Center, and in Wolf's Deli where he met a philosopher waitress. At Carnegie Hall he checked out the archives for a particular event. He visited the Mayor's House – Gracie Mansion, took a Taxi Ride with a Russian Émigré Driver who knew all about Scots History, had a buggy ride round Central Park with a driver who had Mel Gibson and Yoko Ono on board. He went to Penn Station in search of Track 29 which never existed! He dodged a ticket tout, met an official busker, sang at the Metropolitan Opera House (in the foyer), and rode the Staten Island Ferry. He visited the firehouse museum (Peter was also an ex-fireman) and popped into *Sardi's* near Times Square for lunch. His final location was *Asti's* in Greenwich Village where they had the singing waiters. The programme was a joy to make with so many magic moments with Peter's quick reactions to situations.

At Carnegie Hall he talked to the archivist where he found that official programme from his performance which had featured the New York City Police Pipe Band wearing kilts along with their service revolvers which was required by New York City Ordinance. He told the tale of the manager of Carnegie Hall at that time who had found his wife in the arms of her lover and shot them both to death!

The best bit for me in a production sense was the final location at *Astis* in Greenwich Village which was an Italian Restaurant with singing waiters that featured opera music. Customers would include the likes of Ben Kingsley. Peter sang "*Loch Lomond*" and after enjoying a few refreshments sang the *Star Spangled Banner* with the audience joining in.

The magic moment for me came when I was mixing the final part of the show where this anthem had a simple piano accompaniment. To give the ending more impact I remembered some background to *Casablanca* where in the scene in Rick's Cafe the French refugees start singing *La Marseilles* in competition against the Germans *Die Wacht am Rhein*. Producer Hal Wallis instructed that the band accompanying the French singing should not be as seen in the movie but a full scoring orchestra to give it some body. I searched through our production library discs to find a full orchestral version of the *Star Spangled Banner* and struck gold as it was in the same key as Peter's performance so I crossed mixed from this to the full orchestra as the playout of the show.

Shortly after I became Production Controller in July 1981 and Richard Park was made a very able Music Controller I took on responsibility for Religious Affairs! Up until this point it had been the province of someone from our News and Current Affairs Team. The nearest to religion I had ever been was when as a child I had been sent to Sunday school as the token representative of my family. The job involved contacting ministers, priests and rabbis to present our religious spots which consisted of a 60 second *Thought for the Day* in the Breakfast Show and a 90 second *Time Out* just before the midnight news as well as the Sunday morning religious magazine *Down to Earth*. All of these were pre-recorded and I had to arrange studio time and supervise the content of the recordings.

I set out some basic requirements that the morning spots should be inspiring and the evening ones comforting. Although the presenters came from different faiths the content should be of an ecumenical style so all listeners could understand the content. The late nightspots were very important as so many of our listeners lived alone so they would get some comfort from the content. I felt my job was to get the best performances out of the presenters and of course in these days the contributors were paid (in the form of expenses for tax reasons) for their work. Sad to say when Radio Clyde was taken over first by Emap and then Bauer their payments stopped and eventually the morning and evening spots removed thus continuing the relentless path of stripping Clyde of its localness in pursuit of profit.

Quizzes were a great mainstay of our output with listeners competing on the phone for minor cash prizes and sometime major ones like holidays. In my time we always researched our own quiz questions with all answers being checked against at least two sources. The phone calls to the station were free in these days and the competitions fun. I remember on a trip to the States taking a copy of Brewer's Twentieth Century Phrase & Fable Dictionary and coming back with having written over a thousand questions using it as the main source.

For some on air contests we would get a sponsor to provide the prize in exchange for mentions each time it aired while others would be funded by our own Marketing budgets. These could be quite imaginative and run over a period of time. There was one in which the prize was a round the world trip and the questions involved each of the destinations featured. The audience loved it especially as the winner turned out to be a nurse!

Now strange to say but what goes around comes around. A few months after this contest I was out in the car park at our Clydebank HQ on an icy winter day instructing a new production assistant on the Health & Safety aspects of using the radio car. I slipped on the ice and was in agony having ripped the tendons in my left leg. An ambulance was summoned and I was taken to the Western Infirmary where a consultant examined me and decided an immediate operation was required. It turned out that the consultant was married to the nurse who won the round the world trip! Now the NHS (National Health Service) provides excellent care for patients but I couldn't help feel that I was receiving above and beyond from them. I remember declining a general anaesthetic in favour of a local one so I could watch the operation. It was quite fascinating and I felt very detached from the whole thing. After it I had quite a speedy recovery though my left leg was in plaster.

Sad to say Premium Rate phone lines came along and instead of calls to the station being free, listeners were charged for taking part in contests and a share of the revenue from the calls went to the station. While the prize values may have increased this was all paid for by the listeners. With bigger money at stake the gentleness seemed to go from some contests. Potential callers would get angry when they couldn't get through as the prize pot increased. We developed the term GBS – Greedy Bastard Syndrome which reflected the mood of the callers.

When DAB Digital Radio came on the scene in 1999 Radio Clyde's parent company – Scottish Radio Holdings (SRH) – was successful in its licence application to provide services on the Multiplex – the term given to the transmitter that would serve the area. The beauty of the DAB system is that one transmitter can carry up to around 10 services. In addition to relaying its existing FM and AM services SRH decided to set up an entirely new station to provide Country Music 24 hours a day.

There's an interesting history here. Back in the late 90s we were looking for a presenter to host a "New Country" show on Clyde 2. I had listened to one of the RSL (Restricted Licence Service) stations which would come on for a few weeks to provide a special radio service to the community. This one featured Country Music and one of the presenters was an American called Pat Geary, a former Assistant District Attorney from Orange County in California, who had set up home in Scotland and owned a specialist record store in Byres Road, Glasgow. I was impressed by his presenting style and knowledge so I suggested we take him on to host a new show.

Pat Geary was a natural selection to be the Station Manager of the new station and he was assisted by Duncan Leven from our Production Team. The format he devised was very original. To many in the UK the term Country meant Country and Western which invariably featured simple instrumentation and lyrics based on sadness and tragedy. There existed at this time hundreds of artists who were virtually unknown in the UK performing a much more dynamic style of Country with high quality production and lyrical content that was very relevant to modern cultures and lifestyles. Artists like Travis Tritt, Kenny Chesney, Toby Keith, Lonestar, Montgomery Gentry, Tim McGraw, Faith Hill, Jessica Andrews, Blake Shelton, Jamie O'Neal, Keith Urban, Trisha Yearwood, Jo Dee Messina, Lee Ann Womack, Alan Jackson, Brad Paisley and many others were all hit makers on Country Radio in the USA and virtually unknown in the UK. Pat brought the music of these artists and many more to our shores. Within a few months of taking to the air, 3C won worldwide recognition by winning the *Gold Medal for Best Country Format* at the

International Radio Festival of New York. While part of my Production Controller duties at Radio Clyde had been preparing award submissions for various competitions over the years and I had an excellent track record in this, the success for this submission was due to the originality and creativity of Pat Geary.

To play out the service we used a system of automation which would link the music, station identification, promos and voice tracks from the small presentation team. While the playout was live and automated with each segment be it a song, presenter link, promo spot or station identification having its unique number in the Digital Audio Mass Storage System (DAMS), the presenter links were all pre-recorded. Some time blocks were presenter free with just continuous music. The beauty of DAB Digital Radio was the ability to display text information on a small screen on the DAB radios so as a song was playing you would see the title and artist. The initial job of loading up a database of several thousand country songs was a mammoth task for Pat and Duncan to undertake. Each song had to be coded in a manner that would sit in the automation system. The music selection itself was critical. Fundamentally it would be what at the time was termed "New Country" which was a fresh approach to a music style that was radically different from what people thought in the UK was Country. A year or so after the station took to the air I moved in to work on 3C – Continuous Cool Country to replace Duncan who moved back into mainstream services of Clyde 1 and Clyde 2. Most of my duties as Production Controller for Radio Clyde were passed on to others though I still had responsibility for special events and religious broadcasting with Clyde.

At 3C I returned to presenting on radio after an absence of many years. It was a massive learning curve for me. I probably knew around 20 country artists and most of them were in the traditional Country and Western genre which was what 3C was NOT about. No shouts of "Yee Hah!" or pseudo American accents. Our presentation was to be informative, knowledgeable and concise. We built up a reference library on all the artists we featured building up files with cuttings from trade publications and record company handouts. I learned about 300 new to me artists and bands that were all incredibly talented and performed modern country music.

Oh, I made big mistakes in these early days. We went into a booth to record all our links but the music and other items would be dropped in by the playout system when the show went "live". Always be sure of the pronunciation of an artist's name and most especially what sex they are and if you don't know the song, listen to it first before opening your mouth. As we frequently played three or four songs in a row before talking we didn't hear the middle songs at all. My classic booboo was to refer back to a song by an artist called Tracy Byrd saying she gave us a fine performance. Only thing wrong is Tracy Byrd is a 6 ft tall strapping cowboy. After getting a severe justified bollocking from Station Manager Pat, I learned to listen to every track before talking about it.

I loved the modern country scene because the songs were so relevant, creative and often told great stories. And there was a lot of fun. How about "The Big One" by Confederate Railroad – all about farting in church. It wasn't all like that but it had its moments.

Sad to say first Emap failed to capitalise and develop 3C when they took over Scottish Radio Holdings and 3C shut down on 27th March 2007 when new owners claimed that the station did not fit their future plans. Or to put it crudely it didn't fit their portfolio of potential profitability by making radio in the cheapest possible manner.

About a year before that I had been doing a lot of work on the websites for both 3C and Clyde 2. In June of 2006 with the closure of 3C on the cards I was appointed Web Editor for Radio Clyde. As web editor I increased the unique users on the Clyde1.com site from 37,056 (June 06) to 153,681 (May 07), the page impressions from 284,403 (June 06) to 1,077,543 (May 07) and increased the VIP club membership from 13,194 to 22,983.

Part of my responsibilities as Production Controller over the years was to look after the Radio Clyde Archives. We had thousands of magnetic tapes stored in the attic above the Engineering Workshop ranging from all the live music concerts and sessions to every author Alex Dickson had interviewed for his long running weekly 'Authors' programme. We had hundreds of recordings of guest interview specials, outside broadcasts, drama productions and of course sport. I made some of this available to listen to on the website. I received an email request for audio featuring former Glasgow Rangers football star Davie Cooper who had died in 1995. The request came from Graham MacDonald who came originally from Glasgow but now lived in Las Vegas. He was a regular listener online to *Superscoreboard* when it was available through our website. As I had become a frequent visitor to Vegas I decided to look him up on my next trip. We hit it off great style and I became friends with his wife Petra and daughters Lauren and Alex. Lauren was keen on getting into the Music Business so with my experience in the world of publishing I was able to help her with advice and a copy of what was at that time a bible of the business called not surprisingly *This Business of Music*.

In 2007 came the reality check. Within the Bauer Emap regime I had become an expensive animal and the powers that be decided my Web Editor's post was to be closed. Within their corporate structure this was understandable if you took the job I was doing as being purely Web Editor but within Clyde my responsibilities went far beyond the web role. They did offer me a new post of Web Editor but the salary was to be about one third of what I was currently receiving! Managing Director Paul Cooney had called me into his office along with a representative from Bauer's HR Department. Credit to Paul that he had managed to screw out of Bauer an extremely generous redundancy package and once he had outlined it he said I could have a couple of days to consider it. I had been a loyal servant of the company for 34 years and thoroughly enjoyed every moment. Much to his surprise I gave an instant response to say I'll take it and took the opportunity to turn to pastures new and accepted voluntary redundancy.

When I left Clyde I had an idea of a TV documentary series on a group of islands in the North Pacific which I'll explore in *Chapter 20 – Air Mike the Island Hopper*. I started on that with virtually no income except for a couple of consulting jobs for Clyde, a little bit of freelance presentation and the odd travel assignment but I did have a substantial redundancy payoff.

In October 2008 I realised I had to get a full time job so I applied to Travel 2 for the post of Travel Sales Consultant helping Travel Agents package holidays worldwide. While I had no previous experience in the industry my knowledge of overseas countries and of aviation would help.

I must say that though the pay was very poor for the responsibilities you had, the company was great to work for and the people there were fab. The company only dealt with the trade and did not sell direct to the public. Don't go asking me for cheap holidays!

Chapter 20

Air Mike The Island Hopper

America won Guam from Spain on a misunderstanding.
The Romeo and Juliet story of the Lovers Leap.
The significance of the Love Stick on Chuuk.
Stone Money and bare breasts on Yap.
The lifeline air service of Micronesia.

It is perfectly normal for women to go around bare-breasted on the island community of Yap in the Federated States of Micronesia in the North Pacific, but it is considered rude to show bare ankles! That alone could, for some, be the inspiration to plan a ten-part TV series on a group of islands situated in the North Pacific but then there is so much more to discover! It was my passion for aviation rather than bare-breasted women that kicked off my planning for such a TV series.

My proposal was for *Air Mike – The Island Hopper* to be a TV documentary series on the history and contemporary economic status of the islands of Guam, Saipan, Truk (Chuuk), Pohnpei, Kosrae, Kawjalein, Majuro, Palau and Yap. The link for these programmes was the development of air services in the US Pacific Micronesian Islands by an airline affectionately known as *"Air Mike"*. Each show was planned on being one hour long and the common theme would be how the air services provided a critical boost to the economy of the region.

I first discovered the story of the *Island Hopper* while visiting the Smithsonian National Air and Space Museum in Washington DC for my radio documentary *Doing the Continental* in 1985. Their archives had been a goldmine of information on Continental's post-World War 2 operations in the Asia Pacific region, some of which were clandestine. Most will have heard of *Air America* from the 1990 movie of the same name starring Mel Gibson and Robert Downey Jnr. This was about a "secret" CIA operation during the Vietnam War with the front of being a regular civilian airline. What is less well known is that they had a competitor from a company called Continental Air Services, (CAS), founded on September 1st, 1965 with an operating base in Vientiane, Laos, covering the surrounding countries. At that time Continental was already operating to Asia with Trans-Pacific charter flights for the Military Airlift Command (MAC). CAS had a fleet of around 50 aircraft which hauled supplies and passengers into tiny remote airstrips. The operation ran as a wholly owned subsidiary of the parent company for just over ten years till the end of the Vietnam War.

The island groups of Mariana, Caroline and Marshall have a long and fascinating history. In the 16th Century after their discovery by Magellan they became part of the Spanish Empire and in 1688 a Spanish mission was founded on the island of Guam. In 1899 after the Spanish-American War they were purchased by Germany, with the exception of Guam which under the strangest of circumstances became an American possession.

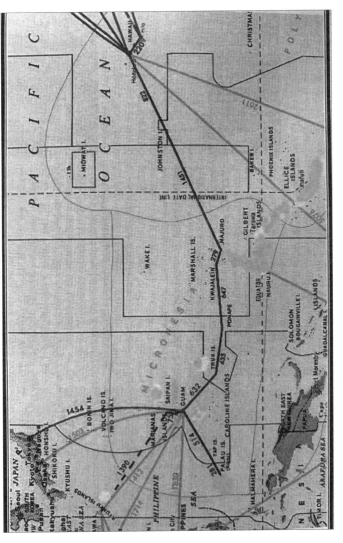

Air Mike Route Map

It was near the start of that war on June 4th, 1898, the *USS Charleston* left Honolulu, Hawaii under the command of Captain Henry Glass with orders to proceed to Guam and take the island. They reached Agana Bay on June 20th, 1898 and came into range of the Spanish fort Santa Cruz. They opened up on the fort with three-pounder guns firing thirteen rounds in four minutes, but there was no response from the fort. A short time later a small vessel carrying the Spanish flag sailed out and approached the *USS Charleston*. On board were Lieutenant Garcia Gutierrez of the Spanish Navy who was in charge of the port and Doctor Romero of the Spanish army who was the Port Health Officer. When they arrived on board they were very friendly perhaps due to the fact that news of the war had not reached their outpost! The Doctor enquired about the health of the crew while the Lieutenant asked if they could borrow some gunpowder to return the salute!

The shocked Spanish officers were brought up to date on the state of affairs in their area of the world and that they were now prisoners of war! Captain Glass discovered that the Spanish military on the island consisted only of 54 Spanish soldiers and 54 Chamorros (native islanders). The two "prisoners" were paroled, with the requirement that they carry a message to the governor that he should come to the vessel as soon as possible.

The governor, Juan Marina, responded that Spanish law forbade him from coming aboard the vessel, but asked the American captain to come to him instead, guaranteeing the captain's safe return. When the governor's letter arrived, it was getting late in the day. The governor was informed that an officer would be sent ashore the next morning.

At 8.30am Lt. William Braunersreuther, the *Charleston's* navigator, went ashore to meet the governor and his party at the village of Piti. As a precaution, landing forces were formed, placed in landing boats and started for the beach. The lieutenant presented a letter from Captain Glass which demanded the surrender of the island within one half-hour of receiving the note, while he verbally reminded the governor that a heavily armed vessel and several transports loaded with troops were waiting offshore. Twenty-nine minutes later, the governor returned with the following reply:

> *"Being without defenses of any kind and without means for meeting the present situation, I am under the sad necessity of being unable to resist such superior forces and regretfully accede to your demands, at the same time protesting against this act of violence, when I have received no information from my government to the effect that Spain is in war with your nation."*

And that is how the United States gained its first possession in the Pacific!

Most of the other islands remained in German hands till the end of World War I when a mandate of the League of Nations granted Japanese jurisdiction which proved to be rather convenient for Japan when they entered World War II on that day of "infamy", 7th December, 1941 with the attack on Pearl Harbour. After World War II the islands were passed to the United States under a mandate from the United Nations and were initially looked after by the US Navy before late in 1949 administration was passed to the US Department of the Interior who set about providing some form of transportation among 84 of the more important of the inhabited islands. This was a mammoth undertaking as the island chain covered a distance of almost 3,000 miles.

The area became known as the Trust Territory of the Pacific and the US Department of the Interior carried out a survey to decide the best method of connecting the islands late in 1950. Bids were invited to operate an air service and on July 1st, 1951 Guam based Transocean Airlines, using four PBY 5A Catalina flying boats modified to carry ten passengers and cargo, won the contract. As the Trust Territory was not yet open to tourists the service was only for the islanders and administrators. The aircraft had been supplied by the navy to Transocean but they had to pay for maintenance, spares, fuel and crews. They managed to survive till July 11th, 1960 when they went bankrupt at which point Pan American Airways was asked to take over the service.

Pan Am at the time could be regarded as the world's most experienced airline with high quality international services. Sadly for the Trust Territories, all they could offer was two ancient Douglas DC 4 aircraft with canvas seats operating to the few islands that had primitive airstrips, and two Albatross Flying Boats for the remaining islands. Service was poor and breakdowns frequent. In the late 1960s the Department of the Interior invited tenders for an improved service and received bids from the incumbent Pan Am, Northwest Airlines, Hawaiian Air, the Recreation Corp of America (of which I can trace no record as an aviation company), and the newly formed Continental Air Micronesia.

The ingenuity of Continental's plans was what won the day for them. In these plans they would form the United Micronesia Development Association, (UMDA), in which they would own 32% and the balance held locally. They made three pledges: they would use jet aircraft – the Boeing twin jet 727-100; they would train Micronesians to become a significant part of their workforce; they pledged to create a tourism industry by building six modern resort hotels. On January 17th, 1968, they won the contract giving Continental what became its first permanent foothold in the Pacific. The time during the Vietnam War spent on the MAC charters and Continental Air Services had paid off. Dominic P Renda, a senior VP from Western Airlines, was appointed as president and he immediately began a program of airfield construction to accommodate the jet services.

Air Micronesia affectionately known by the locals as *Air Mike* operated its inaugural service on May 16th, 1968 when it flew from Okinawa with seven stops –Saipan, Rota, Guam, Truk, Kwajalein, Majuro, and ended up in Honolulu, a distance of 4,300 miles.

In 1969, the tiny island republic of Nauru received a short lived feeder service from Majuro operated by *Air Mike* for just over a year. For its size (8.1 square miles) it was incredibly wealthy down to the simple fact that it was full of shit. Well to be fair the shit was guano, bird droppings, a basic ingredient of the thriving phosphate industry, which was easily strip mined from the island's surface. Unfortunately the guano soon ran out and the state had to turn to various devices to stay alive. These included as a tax haven for money laundering and more recently as an offshore immigration detention facility for the Australian Government. It was a case that for the short lived fortunes of Nauru, the guano shit didn't hit the fan, it just ran out.

All this was just part of my inspiration and initial research. To make it into a proposal for a TV series I had to find a suitable production company and I was fortunate to find that former Radio Clyde News Editor Russell Walker was now a partner in Glasgow based Demus Media. So I set up a meeting with Russell and Managing Director Nick Low at which I outlined my ideas. They reckoned it could be ideal television documentary material for the likes of The Discovery Channel or National Geographic. As they had experience in submitting proposals for commissions they would be able to make my researches fit the requirements of these organisations. I would continue my researches and once complete we would have a shot at getting a commission.

On Monday March 14th, 2005, I set off to Micronesia to sample the Island Hopper myself. I flew from Glasgow via New York to Honolulu with a couple of night's stopover at each point for my first experience of *Air Mike*. It was at 7am on Friday March 18th when I boarded the Boeing 737 flight CO957 to experience how the airline handled the Hopper.

We called in at Majuro (MAJ), Kwajalein (KWA) which is a military base where no photos were permitted, the window blinds had to be pulled down and only military personnel were allowed off or on, then on to Kosrae (KSA), Ponape (PNI) Chuuk formerly known as Truk (TKK) and arriving into Guam (GUM) at 1715, which, as we had crossed the international dateline, was on the following day. As the duty time for the aircrew was around 16 hours they had to carry an extra pilot known as the IRO – International Relief

Officer. In addition to the IRO there was one more critical flight deck crew member – a flight engineer! A Boeing 737 normally has just a two man cockpit crew, however, if the plane had a serious technical problem at one of these remote islands it would be grounded till an engineer was flown out to fix the plane and that could take several days. The engineer would normally sit down the back with the passengers but at each stop he would get off and inspect the aircraft. Essential spares were carried on board.

I had figured out that Guam would be the ideal base for our crew and talked to the Manager of the Hilton about how we could do a deal. Anything was possible except we could not come in peak seasons like Japan's Golden Week when everyone goes on holiday and Japan was their major market.

On March 21st I flew on to Hong Kong via Saipan in the company of Wally Dias, Continental's VP for Sales and Marketing in the region. He was to be my golden contact for the project. He started his career in the finance division of Continental Airlines at corporate HQ in Houston, Texas and in 1993 he moved to Guam to become Director of Marketing then VP for Sales & Marketing. We struck up a great friendship and I was able to obtain a remarkable insight into the *Air Mike* operation along with a list of many contacts that I would follow up either by email or on my next trip.

On my return I spent the next couple of years following up on contacts so I would be able to block out a rough storyboard for the series of ten documentaries. Demus Media could then prepare for potential commissioning companies. I took a further brief trip to Guam in 2007 using KLM flights as far as Hong Kong and then picking up CO910 from Hong Kong to Guam on September 7th. I stayed 3 nights to include a visit to The University of Guam where I spent a day going through their extensive archives on the history of Micronesia.

I was able to complete a first draft of our proposal on the *Air Mike* TV series for Demus Media. Here's an outline of some of what we proposed.

We travel on the Island Hopper as it makes its dawn departure from Honolulu for the fourteen and a half hour flight over 4,000 miles, stopping off at 5 spectacular Micronesian islands on runways hacked out of jungle or perched on coral reefs before reaching its destination of Guam. Running parallel with our flight across the ocean we will look into the history of aviation on the North Pacific and how one man's vision, Dominic P Renda, the President of Continental Micronesia, came to realisation in 1968 and grew to become the essential lifeline to the remote islands with just one aircraft. We will see how *Air Mike* became more than a lifeline for the communities it serves with the growth of tourism to these remote islands.

A second Boeing 727 was added to the fleet in December 1972, which was purchased from the CIA clandestine operation *Air America!* There was a cunning financial arrangement on March 1st, 1977 to bring in revenue whereby Continental sold a Boeing 727 to *Air Mike* for just one dollar then it was leased back to Continental at full price on a 12-year deal to provide an essential revenue stream. This would have been the 3rd aircraft in the *Air Mike* fleet except it never left mainland USA!

On the day of the inaugural flight at one island, the locals were taking bets as the whether the aircraft would make it! The underside of the aircraft had to be coated with Teflon to avoid damage from coral based runways. At some runways the aircraft had to do a fly past first to make sure it was clear of cattle and people, other runways were constructed on slender reefs. These runways on the islands can be very challenging for pilots. On Chuuk and Kosrae they are surrounded by water on three sides while on Majuro the runway occupied a thin strip of land.

The flights today are operated by Boeing 737 aircraft but still have to carry an extra pilot as an IRO – International Relief Officer because of the length duty hours, and a flight engineer still rides in the main cabin.

Despite the challenges, *Air Mike* had a pretty good safety record marred by just one non-fatal crash where the flight engineer's actions proved invaluable for the subsequent investigation. It was November 21st, 1980, while landing heavily at Yap, the aircraft was just an unlucky 13 feet short of the runway when it touched down. The right landing gear was torn off and the aircraft slid along the runway then slid off to the side and into the jungle where it caught fire. The 67 passengers and 6 crew all escaped. The island had only one fire truck and it had to go and refill several times. The flight engineer on realising the aircraft could not be saved instructed the fire crew to concentrate on the area where the "black box" flight recorders were located. They are, in fact, not black in colour but bright orange with one recording the technical information while the other records the last 30 minutes of sounds from within the cockpit including conversations.

The subsequent investigation found out that during the approach to the airport the captain had briefly handed over control to the first officer while he took some photos. When he took back control he had to use a high rate of descent to reach the touchdown point which he misjudged resulting in landing hard and short of the runway. A contributing cause was the fact that he had recently transferred from flying a DC-10 aircraft and was inexperienced in the Boeing 727.

Security is also critical on these flights and at each stop except Kwajalein, half the passengers have to disembark with their carry-on bags while security staff gives a thorough check of the cabin while those remaining on board have to identify all their bags.

Guam is 15 hours ahead of the Eastern seaboard of the USA hence the slogan they use *Guam, Where America's Day Begins!*

There were two particular tourist sites on Guam that I visited. The first was Two Lovers Point, sacred to the Chamorro people. The story behind it could almost be the setting for a Shakespearean tragedy. At the time when Spain ruled Guam, there was a proud family living in Hagatna, the capital city. The father was a wealthy Spanish aristocrat and the mother was the daughter of a great Chamorro chief. The family owned land and were highly esteemed by all, Chamorro and Spanish alike. Their daughter was a beautiful girl, admired by all for her honesty, modesty, and perfectly natural charm. Her beauty bestowed the greatest pride and dignity unto her family.

One day, the girl's father arranged for her to take a powerful Spanish captain as her husband. When the girl discovered this, she was so distraught that she ran from Hagatna all the way to the north of Guam until she found a secluded and peaceful shore. There she met and fell in love with a young warrior from a very modest Chamorro family. He was gentle, with a strong build, long hair just like hers, and had eyes that searched for meaning in the stars.

When the girl's father learned of the two lovers, he grew angry and demanded that she marry the Spanish captain at once. That day at sundown, she stole away to the same high point along the shore, and once again met her Chamorro lover. Her father, the captain, and all the Spanish soldiers pursued the lovers up to the high cliff above Tumon Bay. The lovers found themselves trapped between the edge of the cliff and the approaching soldiers. All the young warrior could do was to warn them to stay back, and the father ordered the soldiers to halt. The lovers then tied their long black hair into a single knot, and acting as if they were entirely alone, they looked deeply into each other's eyes and kissed for the final time. Then they leaped over the high cliff into the roaring waters below. Her father and all who remained rushed to the edge to stare in great anguish. Today the Two Lovers' Point is a popular tourist spot with viewing platforms protected by barriers presumably to stop copycats, and, of course, the mandatory gift shop with duty-free facilities.

The second tourist site was a cave in the jungle. At the end of World War II a few Japanese soldiers held out hidden on the island. The most famous was Sgt. Soichi Yokoi who, after the Americans retook Guam, hid in a cave in the jungle near the village of Talofofo. He was discovered on January 24th 1972 by two villagers, Jesus Duenas and Manuel de Garcia, who managed to subdue him and take him to the local commissioner's office for questioning where he confessed to his identity. He said that he had known in 1952 that the war had ended but had remained hidden with the explanation, "We Japanese soldiers were told to prefer death to the disgrace of being captured alive." On going back to Japan he said, "It is with much embarrassment that I return." He did receive the equivalent of $300 in back pay and a small pension. He died in 1997 at the age of 82.

In my exploration of Guam near the town of Dededo in the North West I came across an arena which was used for cockfighting. It is believed that cockfighting had been brought to Guam in the early 1800s by Filipino immigrants. It's a form of gambling with wagers placed the outcome of fights between roosters. I was cautious in approaching the arena as I suspected that the activity may be somewhat illegal as well as being cruel. There was no fight on but I was invited in to look around the arena. As there was quite a large Filipino population in the area the nature of the housing and lifestyle was somewhat different to the rest of the island. They had arrived just after World War II when the US Navy constructed houses for immigrant labourers who were helping in Guam's development. Filipinos at that time made up around 26% of the population. This area was certainly avoided by the island tours.

I never got a chance to explore the Island of Chuuk, the home to the Love Stick. This is not what you might be thinking but then how do I know what your thoughts are? I would reckon it is more symbolic than euphemistic. Before we get into the ritual of the Love Stick we take a brief peek at the history of Chuuk which was known as Truk prior to 1990. Well if India can change the names of its key cities why not Micronesia? The inhabitants are known as Chuukese but despite the presence of the Love Stick, the Ricky Lee Jones song *Chuck E's in Love* has no connection with this Micronesian state!

So what about the romantic history of that *Love Stick*? In past years an island man would carve his personal notches on the *Love Stick* and let his would-be sweetheart feel it. For clarification the *Love Stick* was a piece of wood and not a euphemistic term for his penis! At night, *Love Stick* in hand, he would kneel beside the thatch wall opposite where the girl lay sleeping, poke the stick through the wall and entangle her long hair, hopefully awakening her without awakening her family. The silent language of the *Love Stick* began when the girl put her fingers around the shaft's notches and identified the owner. I reckon if I tried that I would end up being subject to a court restraining order!

The one island I really wanted to experience but never had the chance was Yap, famed for its Stone Money and bare-breasted women!

The Stone Money, known as Rai are large donut-shaped, carved disks of calcite which vary in size, the smallest known one is 3 inches in diameter. The value is based on both the stones size and its history due to the difficulty involved in obtaining them. Nowadays, as this money supply is fixed, the islanders know who owns which piece but they tend not to move them when ownership changes as many are very difficult to move around. The largest would take about twenty men to do the job.

Surprisingly, Stone Money is still legal tender on Yap but the United States Dollar is used for everyday transactions. Just imagine the excess baggage charge if you had to carry the Stone Money on your flights! The stone disks are used for more traditional or ceremonial exchange like in marriages, transfer of land title or as compensation for damages suffered by an aggrieved party.

As for the bare-breasted women, it's part of their cultural heritage and traditional dress style. Not everyone goes around like this but you will still find a fair number respecting this fine tradition. I was told that while they don't mind bearing their breasts they really like to cover their ankles.

So how did my attempts to obtain a commission from one of the major TV companies go? I'm still waiting, wishing and hoping!

Chapter 21

Circus Circus Las Vegas

The Ringmaster's Club had me hooked.
Do they send the elephant instead of the limousine?
Hieroglyphs surprisingly accurate.
How to make money from a casino – own it!
The Mormons and the Mafia Mob.

Chance plays a major part in any casino experience. It was by chance I happened to be staying in Las Vegas at a Travelodge next door to Circus Circus on one of my early visits to the west coast of the USA when I was following up on some music publishing interests. I had driven there from Los Angeles and it was just a night stop. I thought I would have a little play on one of the slot machines in the main casino and as I happily parted with a few quarters into a device I wasn't very sure about, I heard a scream coming from above. I looked up there were trapeze artistes performing in the roof area! Call me stupid if you like, but at that point I realised why the casino was called Circus Circus with acrobats doing their stunts in an overhead arena.

While I was playing I was approached by a sweet Casino Host and asked if I would like to join the Ringmasters

Donya Stole VIP Host at Circus Circus

Club. She explained that as a member I would receive a membership card to earn points which could be used towards complimentary meals and even free stays. While I didn't think I was going to be a regular Vegas visitor (how wrong I was) I signed up on the basis of you never know when you'll be back.

How these loyalty cards work is relatively simple. You insert your card into the slot machine before you start playing and it will log your play into a central database. The casino is able to monitor each player and track down any they think could be encouraged to play more by special attention such as VIP Services. The number of points you earn will depend on the value to the casino (often referred to as "the house") of your play. Each slot machine works on the principle of a house "hold" but the amount of "hold" varies from machine to machine and the value of the bet. On higher bets the house hold tends to be lower. So what do I mean by "hold"? While every play is random the machine is set to give an average payback. This can bet set to anything between stingy amounts like 80% to a generous 99%. Most tend to be around 90% which would mean over a period of time if you started with $100, you are likely to get on average just $90 back once you had put through that initial $100.

It was a few months later that I returned to Las Vegas and decided to stay at Circus Circus for a few nights. I'd done some research and found myself understanding many of the games on the slot machines. There are some basic rules of survival. The house always wins, so only gamble with what you are prepared to lose. Remember, someone has to pay for all the bright lights and "free" drinks as well as the complimentary rooms – you! Quit while you are ahead and be happy with a small win rather than chasing that big one. On this visit I was moving around trying out many different slots and having a degree of success. I also learned certain matters of etiquette like always tip your waitress or you'll probably not see her again for a long time. Drinks are free if you are actively playing a slot machine. While most wins then were paid in coins by the machines, larger amounts had to be paid by a slot attendant and a small tip was in order for them.

It appeared that my play was sufficient to attract the attention of VIP Services and a representative tracked me down to the machine I was playing and advised me that I was now entitled to their benefits which included my own VIP Host, free nights and other special privileges like a "line pass" for queues at the buffet. Yes, they had me well and truly hooked! Your card also racked up "comp" dollars which could be used in restaurants or towards hotel rooms. They would also provide you with a "free" limo service to and from the airport but I soon found out that this was not actually free, they would take the cost out of your comps! I had this weird thought that as it was Circus Circus, they would send an elephant to pick you up! Your comp dollars could also be used for show tickets at sister casinos. This became quite useful as Circus Circus

Enterprises expanded into the Mandalay Resort Group but more on this later.

Back in September, 1978 at Radio Clyde I had hired Magi Sloan as a Production Assistant. I'd been impressed by her qualifications in Dramatic Studies at the Royal Scottish Academy of Music and Drama – RSAMD (now known as the Royal Conservatoire of Scotland). At Radio Clyde she did an excellent job of looking after our Music Library and supply of copyright information to P.R.S – the Performing Right Society as well as assisting in our drama productions. In June 2009, she was made redundant at Radio Clyde so she put her drama skills to use working on TV and film productions in a variety of roles. She also developed her interest in Egyptology (the study and understanding of ancient Egypt). She loved flying and together we would do crazy day trips to European destinations on holiday charter aircraft just for the fun of the flights. We would find flights with a couple of last minute empty seats going real cheap and head out on them for that crazy day trip. We did two trips to Geneva. On the first one we just stood at the top of the plane steps on arrival, looked at the falling snow and went back to our seats and back home. On the second trip we actually got off the plane, ran round Duty Free for chocolate and straight back on to the aircraft. The passenger sitting next to Magi thought she must be super rich flying all the way to Switzerland just to buy chocolate!

Magi at that time did not share my love of America but I figured she might change her mind if she came with me on a little excursion out to Las Vegas, and in particular give me her opinion of the Luxor Hotel and Casino which was Egyptian themed. So using my Frequent Flyer miles with Continental I booked the two of us in Business Class to fly out on Friday, February 8th, 2013, from Glasgow to Las Vegas via New York. It was a magnificent plan especially as I hadn't let on that we would be travelling Business Class. To quote Robert Burns, Scotland's National Bard, *"the best laid schemes o' mice an' men gang aft agley"* meaning quite simply no matter how carefully a project is planned, something will go wrong with it. And it did, big style!

The night before we were due to leave I was at my desk in Travel 2 where I was now working as a travel trade consultant. I did a routine check on my flights on Galileo, the computer reservations system (CRS), to make sure all was OK. Horror! There had been a massive snowstorm on the East Coast of the USA. All airports were shut and all flights cancelled! I quickly phoned Continental's Priority Line in the USA and much to my pleasant surprise got through after just a five minute wait. An extremely helpful agent worked with me on the how to reach Las Vegas from anywhere in the UK by avoiding the East Coast. She found two possibilities out of London going the following morning but we would have to make our own way to London. One was going on the nonstop to Los Angeles and connecting to Las Vegas and the other was going to San Francisco and then Vegas but there were only two seats left on either sets of flights. I preferred via San Francisco which turned out to be a wise choice as we discovered later that the Los Angeles aircraft had been diverted to Shannon in Ireland due to a technical issue and the passengers had to overnight there! I quickly booked us on to the 0800 British Airways flight from Glasgow to London Heathrow which would give us time to catch the Continental flight to San Francisco.

Our flight from London was delayed due to a blocked toilet but eventually it departed. Their operations team were faced with the pilots running out of duty hours, so they reckoned on the large aircraft they would manage with one less lavatory even though the flight was full.

We arrived in Las Vegas late that evening and the next day I introduced Magi to my VIP hosts. She found a slot machine *"Pharaoh's Fortune"* which she loved and almost adopted. Magi is a very sensible gambler and plays the slots just for fun rather than trying to win. She had a small fixed amount for playing, and once it was gone, she would stop. She did manage to make it last a long time just one coin at a time!

We took *The Deuce,* the double-decker bus that runs along the Las Vegas Strip 24 hours a day, down to The Luxor and I let Magi explore. Much to my pleasant surprise she was full of praise for the accuracy of the Egyptian themed building and artefacts! The hieroglyphs were correct! It looks like I had a Vegas convert. From that point on she would try and make at least one trip a year to Circus Circus for a slot tournament.

Many casinos in Las Vegas operate promotional slot tournaments. These vary from casino to casino so for clarity here I'll just talk about how they work at Circus Circus. The tournament runs over a couple of days. VIP members of the Players Club (formerly Ringmasters) could take part for free, but non VIPs had to pay a $50 registration fee. There is something in the region of $50,000 total in prizes, but check the small print. The prizes are not in pure cash but in free slot play to the prize value amount. You can only get cash once you had "laundered" the prize money through the slot machines. You can cash out at any point, but only your winnings will come out in cash, any residue will remain on your Players Club card for you to use on another machine. The Tournament top prize would be $10,000 in free slot play, with scaled prizes right down to 130th place which receive just $50.

There are usually four rounds – two on each day of the tournament. There is a bank of around fifty identical slot machines which are installed in the specially constructed tournament area to allow for fifty participants at a time. The number of sessions per round will depend on how many people sign up for the tournament but I reckon they normally have around 250 participants, so to accommodate them all, they have up to five sessions for each round. You can't pick the machine for your sessions, they are allocated by drawing a number as you line up to play. Each session will last 15 minutes at which you repeatedly hit the "play" button to operate the machine. Some folk hit the play button real hard while others have a soft touch but it makes no difference. At the end of each session the tournament hosts collect the individual scores. They also have an additional money maker for the casino with the ability for participants to "Better Your Odds" by playing an additional round at the end of the first day, but you have to buy in to this for an extra fee of around $40. If you did this, only the top four scores are counted out of your five rounds for the tournament. For participants it's a fun social occasion as you get to meet so many players from far and wide. The tournaments are also themed whereby the area is decorated and the hosts dress up in fancy costumes.

So, how does the casino expect to shell out $50,000 with very little revenue from the tournament itself? You have to look at the big picture. They know on average how much they expect to make out of each participant during the time of their stay at the casino and it may surprise you. If each player just lost $200 during their time at the casino that would cover it. As participants must be members of the Players Club it is a good recruiting tool. The tournament session times spread throughout the two days of the event result in players spending the in-between time in the casino on other slots, and the event itself attracts customers. They wouldn't do it if it wasn't a big money maker but it does contribute to the fun experience for participants. Remember – don't gamble to make money, just have fun. The only way to make money in a casino is to own it!

The ownership of Circus Circus has a fascinating history steeped in the bad old days when the Mafia had a major hand in the operation of Las Vegas, but first a brief early history of what became known as "Sin City". The name Las Vegas, which means in Spanish 'the meadows', came from the Spanish explorer and merchant Antonio Mariano Armijo famed for leading the first commercial caravan party in 1829-1830 between Abiquiu, Nuevo Mexico and San Gabriel Mission in Alta California. In 1844 explorer John Charles Fremont as a Major in the US Army set up a base at the Las Vegas Springs establishing a clandestine fort in preparation for a war with Mexico. Fremont Street in Downtown Las Vegas is named after him. In 1855, William Bringhurst led a group of 29 Mormon missionaries from Utah to the Las Vegas Valley and built an adobe fort which they abandoned in 1857 but the Mormons were to return. The next key development was the arrival of the San Pedro, Los Angeles and Salt Lake Railroad in 1905 and on May 15th Las Vegas was officially founded as a city. Shortly after that, the State of Nevada became the last Western state to outlaw gaming. It even forbade the western custom of flipping a coin for the price of a drink! This remained in force until 1931 when the Nevada state legislature legalised gambling as it would be profitable for local businesses who expected to take advantage of the construction of the nearby Boulder Dam (now Hoover Dam). In reply to this the federal government restricted the movement of dam workers to Las Vegas.

While ethnic organised crime had been involved in some of the operations at the hotels, the Mafia bosses had been excluded by hard bitten local families who managed to keep them out. Mafia head honchos Bugsy Siegel and Meyer Lanksy poured money through locally owned banks as a cover to build the Flamingo in 1946.

The Bank of Las Vegas led by Edward Parry Thomas was the first bank to lend money to the casinos. Thomas, a devout Mormon, first arrived in Las Vegas from Salt Lake City in 1954 with $250,000 start up cash from Mormon investors. The International Brotherhood of Teamsters through its President Jimmy Hoffa began lending money to casinos from their pension fund. The casinos to benefit from this included the Sahara, Sands, New Frontier, Showboat, Riviera, and the Tropicana. For the full story behind the Mafia connections with Las Vegas a visit to the Mob Museum in Downtown is a must.

American developer, hotelier and casino owner Jay Sarno from Missouri opened Circus Circus on October 18, 1968. Sarno had made his money through building Caesars Palace which had taken four years and was financed with Mob money through Jimmy Hoffa's Teamsters Union Pension Fund. Sarno had a pattern of wild spending which didn't please his partners. He fell out with one of his partners in Caesars, Nathan Jacobson, and in 1967 bought a tract of land across from the Riviera with plans to open a hotel casino. He had trouble attracting investors so he removed the hotel part from his plans. His idea was to theme the casino on lines of a circus within a Roman circus, but he soon dropped the Roman aspect but kept the name Circus Circus and it opened on October 17th, 1968.

At a cost of $15 million, it consisted of a giant pink and white circus tent with a casino but no hotel attached so it was not able to attract high rollers (big spenders). It was a crazy place where trapeze artistes did somersaults above the craps tables. Sideshow barkers tempted guests to midway attractions along the inside walls of the massive tent. It may have been like a circus but it certainly was not for kids, only for adults to act like kids.

By this time the Federal Organised Crime Task Force was having a major effect on the Mob in Las Vegas but it was to take almost twenty years before the Mafia involvement was totally removed.

With a $23 Million loan from the Teamsters Union Pension Fund Sarno added a hotel in 1971. After investigation into organised crime connections, Sarno sold Circus Circus to William Bennett and William Pennington for $25 million in 1974. This deal was to be the foundation of one of the largest gambling empires in the world.

Behind the deal was the Mormon banker E. Parry Thomas of the Valley Bank of Nevada. Bennett and Pennington had been trying unsuccessfully, with his help, to buy several different casinos including the Landmark and the Four Queens. Then Thomas suggested they should go for Circus Circus.

Bennett had been studying the operation for a few months before the purchase went through and was convinced that bad management and employee theft were ruining the business. On the day of takeover he fired all the top managers and replaced them with a crew that had been selected by Angel Naves who he had brought in as his new manager of Circus Circus along with Tony Alamo as his assistant. They had both worked together in Lake Tahoe at the Sahara Tahoe Casino. Bennett then moved quickly to redesign the casino. He kept the circus performers but moved them and the midway games to the second floor with a roof covering most of the casino below. They were concerned that the midway was not doing the kind of business they expected so they hired a carnie (carnival) expert from Santa Monica Pier to take charge of operations. They noticed a change in the casino's clientele. Parents were coming into the casino with their kids but sending them upstairs to the midway while they played on the casino floor as children are not allowed in gaming areas by law.

Casinos in Vegas were always after the high rollers but not so for the new Circus Circus. Bennett thought that they were going after the wrong crowd and decided he was going to give them the best value for their dollar. While other casinos allocated just 30 per cent of their floor space to slot machines, he reversed it to 70 per cent for slots, and he calibrated them so they paid out jackpots more frequently than other casinos in Vegas. He set his machines to pay out 97.4 per cent which meant that his slots had the loosest hold of any in Las Vegas. Now it is illegal for a casino owner to know in advance when a slot machine is going to pay a jackpot, but they can determine how many jackpots are going to be paid within a random number of handle pulls.

Bennett introduced a single combined bank of eight machines which in addition to paying out their own jackpots of $1,000 also had an extra jackpot of $8,000 available across the eight. He reduced the hotel room rates down to $18 when the average price on The Strip was $60. They were swamped with bookings so he then set up a system by providing free transportation to off-strip hotels at the same rate. This meant a very busy casino whose customers had to be fed, so he installed the cheapest in town all-you-can-eat buffet. By the end of the first year they were making so much money that they were able to add a 15 storey hotel tower with 795 more rooms. Expansion in Las Vegas was to follow. In June 1990, Circus Circus Enterprises opened the Excalibur with more than 4,000 rooms which was at that time the largest hotel in the world.

In November 1991 they announced the construction of the Luxor which opened on October 14th 1993. In 1994 Bill Bennett resigned as Chairman of Circus Circus Enterprises as the company continued its expansion. In 1999 they opened the Mandalay Bay Resort and Casino and Circus Circus Enterprises changed its name to the Mandalay Resort Group. In 2005 MGM Resorts, owners of the MGM Grand and several other casinos in Vegas and worldwide, merged with the Mandalay Resort Group.

Sad to say that Circus Circus, where everything had evolved from, became the orphan child of the corporate structure. It did not fit in to the grand scheme of things and while continuing to be a cash cow for the MGM group, little investment was forthcoming. Parts of the catering were then franchised out. The most annoying thing for me was the Pink Pony 24 hour restaurant which had become the Casino Cafe then was leased out to become Vince Neil's Tatuado but no longer operated 24 hours a day. I like to be able to breakfast at any time of day or night. In 2019 MGM Resorts sold Circus Circus to Phil Ruffin for $825 million.

They used to have a saying "what happens in Vegas stays in Vegas". That was certainly true when it came to my money but I always stayed in control so I knew just how much my "fun" was costing me. On one occasion my VIP host showed me on a spreadsheet just how much I had gambled and lost over a ten year period. I was not surprised at the figures as they matched what I thought I had spent so I was in control. I thought it was a very responsible action on the part of my host to make sure I was within my limits.

Chapter 22

On the Fly

Murphy's Laws of Hub Operation.
Suitable for upgrade or friend of the gate agent?
Hooters Air go bust!

When the gate agent at the airport puts a "FAT" tag on your bag, they are not passing judgement on your body size but simply stating your destination is Fresno Air Terminal in California. Fun facts like this were invaluable for me when, in 2000, I started an occasional column *"On The Fly"* in Scottish Travel Agents News – STAN, a weekly magazine distributed to the Scottish Travel Trade. I did it for fun and to keep my hand in on aviation journalism. Here's a small selection of the material I used in the column.

Airlines had developed "Hub and Spoke" operations whereby mainly in the USA, they would concentrate their operations on several hubs providing connecting flights to a multiplicity of destinations that would not normally have enough traffic to merit non-stop services. In theory this was fine but in practice I found the following guidelines to be *Murphy's Laws of Hub Operation* to apply.

The distance between connecting gates is inversely proportional to the connecting time.

The earlier your aircraft arrives at the hub, the longer you have to wait for a gate.

In the interest of fuel economy, gates nearest the terminal will only be used when all other gates are full, and then they will use a tow tractor to take you to your gate further delaying your arrival.

Airbridges linking the terminal to the aircraft door only become inoperative on late arrivals with tight connections.

Long lines only exist at check in when you have bags to check. There are no lines when you just have carry-on bags.

If a connection can be held, it won't.

Flights are only cancelled when it looks like a late departure is endangering an on time record.

The clarity of messages broadcast over the airport PA system are in inverse proportion to the importance of the message.

Through flights (ones with the same flight number for arrival and onward departure to con customers into thinking they will stay on the plane) will have a change of aircraft to a completely different type from a gate at the connecting airport that is the furthest distance from your arrival gate.

A highly sophisticated computerised study of passenger flow is constantly updated to plan gate assignments to ensure the maximum number of passengers have to walk the longest distance to get to their connecting flight.

If you are running late for a flight, it will depart from the farthest gate within the terminal.

If you arrive very early for a flight, it inevitably will be delayed.

If you must work on your flight, you will experience turbulence as soon as you touch pen to paper.

If you are assigned a middle seat, you can determine who has the seats on the aisle and the window while you are still in the boarding area. Just look for the two largest passengers.

The crying baby on board your flight is always seated next to you.

The best-looking woman or guy on your flight is never seated next to you.

The less carry-on luggage space available on an aircraft, the more carry-on luggage passengers will bring aboard.

Flights never leave from Gate #1 at any terminal in the world.

There was an old nursery rhyme that went on the lines of "*Oh dear, what can the matter be, three old ladies were stuck in the lavatory, they were there from Monday to Saturday but nobody knew they were there*". We used to use the term apocryphal to describe a story of doubtful authenticity widely circulated as being true. This was too big a word for the simple folk to whom the Internet was the bible so they came up with "Fake News". One such story from that great source of unreliable and unchecked information concerned a rather large American lady flying on one of these very nice modern jets which happened to have the latest high tech vacuum operated toilet. According to this "story" she made the big mistake of remaining seated while flushing the toilet and so became vacuum-sealed to the bowl! The flight crew were unable to release her so she had to remain "seated" till the aircraft landed and a ground engineer could board to disconnect the system. It was, of course, totally untrue. Apparently the alleged "incident" was from a staff training exercise in Scandinavia.

In the very early days of aviation when aircraft were unpressurized, the on-board toilet was a bucket and disposal was discretional through an open window or door. Not so in modern planes where it goes straight into a storage tank on board.

Some tales do have credibility. There was a small Scottish airline with the flight deck open to the main cabin. The pilot allegedly boarded dressed in civilian clothes and joined the passengers in the cabin. He then drummed his fingers impatiently and said, "I can't wait any longer", and went to the pilot's seat and took off. He is probably the same chap who put the aircraft on autopilot and walked down the back with two long bits of string and asked a passenger to help him steer the plane while he went to the toilet! Then there was the pilot who walked a blind passenger's guide dog for exercise during a refuelling stop.

So what's the secret behind these Airport Codes? We now know that FAT is not for obese people but a straightforward logic for Fresno Air Terminal. IATA – the International Air Transport Association is where these codes originate on consultation with the airports to avoid duplication.

Sometimes check-in agents are tempted to tell annoying customers to GTF. If they tagged a bag there it would end up in Great Falls in Montana. New York's LGA Airport is named after a former Mayor of the city, Fiorella H. LaGuardia. In Orlando, Florida the logical code ORL belongs to the local executive airport while the main international one is MCO. This is derived from McCoy Air Force Base, the former occupant of the property. MSY for New Orleans you might think has something to do with the Mississippi River but it actually comes from the former site of Moisant Stock Yards. Nashville, the home of country music, has the code BNA named after Colonel Harry Berry who helped build the original airport. There is actually a record label called BNA.

Travel Agents have to deal with geographically and mentally challenged customers especially when they happen to be aides to politicians. Not surprisingly the following are all from the USA.

There was one who said they wanted to go to Rhino in New York. "No such city" said the agent. It turned out they wanted to go to Buffalo. The customer responded with "I knew it was a big animal!". A senator's aide called for costs on a package trip to Hawaii and when they got the price she asked if it wouldn't be cheaper to fly to California then take the train to Hawaii! Then there was one who wanted to fly to "Pepsi-Cola" in Florida. Yes, you've guessed that Pensacola was the real thing.

Tipping is such a major issue in the USA where many workers have to rely on tips to make up their wages. In a restaurant where you have a great meal you'll leave a decent tip. So what about airlines? Flight attendants do not get great wages but if you get great service there is something positive you can do that they will appreciate far more than simply money. Take a note of their name and flight number and write to the airline about the outstanding service you received. The airlines get so many letters of complaint that one of praise makes a big difference to that employee as it will go on their staff record.

According to legend long before airlines could track the loyalty of their best customers, the best way to get an upgrade was to dress smart, present a nice smile to the check-in agent and politely ask if there was any chance of an upgrade. The agent had the power to mark on the manifest the code SFU – suitable for upgrade. Nowadays with sophisticated revenue management systems in place, upgrades really depend on two factors. How much did you originally pay for the flight and how high are you in the Frequent Flyer Scheme? Don't expect to move from a seat priced at $100 in deep discount Economy to one at $2,000 in First Class. There used to be one acronym in the world of upgrades that you'll not see on any manifests and that is FOGA, but it has been known to work, Friend Of the Gate Agent!

In flight announcements can be the source of some fun. There was the camp BA steward who said during the life jacket demonstration, "and a whistle to attract the attention of passing sailors".

Flying can be a bit of a Boom or Bust enterprise. On October 4th, 1983 the first Hooters Restaurant opened its doors in Clearwater, Florida with a mission to deliver to the world a unique customer experience in a fun sport-enthused atmosphere. Twenty years on from that opening, the franchise that described itself as a "delightfully tacky yet unrefined experience" moved into the airline business. While the conservative faction in the industry might hold its hands up in horror at the thought they should remember that it was only a few years earlier that the industry was shaken up by the Virgin invasion.

Hooters Air used Boeing 737 aircraft with a flight deck crew in traditional pilot uniforms. In the cabin there were three flight attendants in khaki pants and orange "Hooters Air" polo shirts along with two Hooters Girls in traditional Hooters Restaurant uniforms. The trained flight attendants would be primarily there for your safety while the other two would assist with food and beverage. The airline operation of Hooters lasted three years when intense competition in the industry mainly on pricing forced them to cease operation. Some would say that they went bust, but that's unfair as busts were a key feature.

I managed to sprinkle a selection of aviation humour throughout these STAN columns. Here's a selection.

You know it's a bad sign if the insurance vending machine next to the check-in desk has a sign saying "sold out".

I wouldn't say the aircraft was underpowered but when you turned on the overhead air vent you could feel the plane slowing down.

I wouldn't say the plane was old, but we stopped at Newcastle to take on coal.

They should make aircraft out of the same material as the black box as it always survives crashes.

On low frills airlines it's not buckle your seat belts but fasten your Velcro. In an emergency they rent you oxygen. Instead of movies they show you trailers of films being shown by other airlines. There's no tea or coffee but the stewardess has her own lemonade stand.

It's a bit much when you go back to the airport to see if they have found your lost bags and the agent is wearing your clothes.

Then there was the pilot who accidentally left the PA on when he thought he was just talking to his co-pilot an announced "the first thing I'm going to do is take a crap then grab that new stewardess". The lead flight attendant rushed towards the cockpit but a sweet old lady grabbed her arm and said "there's no need to hurry, he's not gone to the toilet yet".

Then there's the whole world of Marketing Speak. Here are some explanations of what the airlines really mean when they say.....

PASSENGER DEMAND – We wanted to close the route the passengers really liked to put them on the route we couldn't fill

INCREASED CAPACITY – We have cut the legroom

NEW PRICING INITIATIVE – The fares are going up

RESTRICTIONS APPLY – The fares are going up

SOME RESTRICTIONS APPLY – The fares are still going up

CODESHARE CONVENIENCE – We make more money

DIRECT FLIGHT – via

CONVENIENT CONNECTION – Convenient for us as we make more money

COMMERCIAL ALLIANCE – You don't know who you are flying with

FARES WAR – Once we kill the competition we'll get the fares back up

SPECIAL FARES – Please change you booking so we can make more money

SERVICE ENHANCEMENTS – We have found a cheaper way of doing it

IMPROVED SCHEDULE – We've made the block times longer so we can be on time more often

FREQUENT FLYER BONUS –We know your name, we know your habits, the bonus is we can put up our prices to fit your habits

APPROPRIATE CATERING – Peanuts!

WE WELCOME COMPETITION – Bastards!

I did a rewrite of many of the columns for the American market when the Campbell Express, the local weekly paper in the City of Campbell (just next to San Jose), carried about sixty columns over a two year period from 2013.

Chapter 23

21st Century Travel

Lounging around the world Polaris style.
Australian snake in the mouth.
A pokie is not a sexual act.
Enlightenment through beer.
Over the North Pole in search of the sanity clause.
The Lucky Shag may surprise you.
I fall for a camel called Darcy.
Grilled by the Feds in Las Vegas.

My passion for travel went into overdrive in the 21st century. I did like to turn left when I boarded most aircraft because that's where Business or First Class was located and I felt comfortable sitting near the driver. There were two frequent flyer schemes I concentrated on to keep my status up. They were United Airlines/Star Alliance and Emirates Skywards. Both gave me access to their club lounges which was a major plus on any journey with free food, drinks and in many cases showers. In some way the two airlines were deadly rivals yet the combination suited my travel needs. To get lounge access you had to be travelling in Business or First or having a frequent flyer status with entitlement. To understand the value of this,

Emirates occasionally offer paid lounge access if space is available but this is in the region of $100 US per passenger!

Pre-flight Snack in Emirates LA Lounge

In the early part of the new millennium, Emirates was not yet on my radar as their service out of Glasgow did not start till 2005. I was still milking my Northwest Million Miler status to travel out to Thailand via the USA. In my worldwide travels over the years I have had only two major catastrophic events that had severe impact on my plans. The second was the Covid-19 pandemic in 2020 which I'll address much later. The first was the September 11th 2001 terrorist attacks in the USA when all flights were grounded in America.

I had used KLM flights from Glasgow on September 2nd, 2001, via Amsterdam then picked up Northwest flights via

Detroit, Las Vegas, Tokyo, and on to Bangkok Dom Muang Airport arriving on 5th September. Northwest had started a service between Las Vegas and Tokyo so I wanted to try it out. I think they were trying to appeal to Japanese big spending gamblers but the route did not last long. Could it be the Japanese didn't have Yen for it?

It was to be my usual trip of experiencing the pleasures of Pattaya but on the evening of September 11th as I was walking back to my hotel, images of the horrors unfolding in the USA were appearing on TV. The desires for any kind of entertainment disappeared rapidly. The next morning I checked the flight situation and the chances of returning to the UK via the USA were impossible for the foreseeable future. I figured I had to find another way home so I called my travel agent in Scotland who advised that while they could issue me a one-way ticket back home it would be incredibly expensive. I would be better looking for a local Thai agent who would have access to discounted one-way flights. I managed to get booked on to British Airways non-stop to London in economy (World Traveller) class at a discounted fare. Not surprisingly, security at Dom Muang Airport for the flight was extreme. You had a full personal body search and you had to empty the contents of your carry-on bag for detailed scrutiny. The fallout from 9/11 was pretty severe and one particular aspect was access to the fight deck during any trip was denied. I had been so lucky in the past being able to join the drivers especially when making documentaries.

In June 2010 Mexico was calling me, not by phone but by a desire to check out the massive resort area of Cancun and in particular what you would get for "all inclusive". I also wanted an opportunity to practice my limited

Spanish. Strange to say I found my linguistic ability tended to be enhanced by the amount of alcohol I consumed. My favourite tipple was *Cuba Libre* (Bacardi and Coke) and when I got *"muy borracho, yo hablo mucho Espanol"*, Dutch courage overcame any conversational inhibitions. In my broadcasting days as a joke I used to thank my producer Ron Bacardi!

US Air at that time operated a non-stop flight from Glasgow to Philadelphia and an onwards service to Cancun. The aircraft was a rather old Boeing 757 and had an in-flight entertainment system of just a couple of TV monitors hanging in the ceiling in economy. I suspected it was so old it could have been operated on the Baird system. Despite all the technology available on flights today, I always have a good book just in case the in-flight entertainment system is inoperative. At that time US Air was a member of the Star Alliance so I could earn miles on the trip and I chose to use miles to upgrade the sector from Philadelphia to Cancun. That proved to be a waste of valuable miles. US Air were not renowned for their catering and it was severely lacking on my three hour trip down to Cancun and there was no functioning in-flight entertainment.

I had booked to stay at the Blue Bay Club, Puerto Juarez, which is four miles north of Cancun in a quiet beachside location. The hotel is now known as the Al Ritmo Cancun Resort and Waterpark. Here's a lesson in booking transfers. Always book a private one unless you want to be crammed into a full minibus with hot sweaty smelly passengers in tropical heat. There were nineteen of us on the transfer trip and eight stops on the way, most of them in and around an area known as the Hotel Zone which has over twenty luxury mega resorts. Needless to say I was the last to be dropped off in a very sweaty and stinky condition. After that, things became much more agreeable with a nice room, reasonable buffet style food and swim up bar. But the most fun I had was at the theatre/restaurant which for three nights a week put on their own amateur musical extravaganzas with the hotel staff as the cast. The best was their version of the *Pirates of the Caribbean* in which they managed to have a remarkably good lookalike for Johnny Depp.

While the pay working in the travel trade may be lousy the perks can sometimes be pretty stunning. It's essential to have personal experience of the products you sell so you may be sent out on fam (familiarisation) trips to all parts of the world. It is important to understand that these trips are not free holidays. You have to work darn hard learning about what a destination/country has to offer. You may have an itinerary that has ten hotel inspections in one day and that can be pretty exhausting with very little free time. By the time you return from one of these trips you need a holiday!

On 30th May 2011, Travel 2 sent me on an educational trip to Australia to attend an event called Corroberee Europe being held in Darwin, the Capital of the Northern Territories. Tourism Australia organises these events for travel agents around the world. It would consist of a three day workshop hosted by around 90 different suppliers with ten minute sessions at each one. There would be in the region of 250 attendees who for this event had been flown in from all over Europe. In the evenings there would be major functions at which you would socialise with all the suppliers. At the conclusion of the workshops we would split up into small groups each given an Australian name like Cockatoo or Kangaroo and head off for a five day familiarisation trip to one of Australia's fine tourism regions.

This was going to be my second Australian trip having been out to Sydney two years earlier. The language I knew of Australia would be based around sayings like *fair dinkum to toss another shrimp on the barbie!* While that might be fine for Aussie slang, it would not be a true historical representation of the spoken word. It's estimated that in 1788 when European settlers first hit Australia's shores there were around 250 different languages spoken by the Aboriginal, or as they are known today, Indigenous people. Learning a bit of the native language would be impossible but at least I could study a bit of history and the flight out with Qantas from London via Singapore to Darwin helped me big style. On the in-flight entertainment system I put aside all the latest movies available in favour of an audio channel giving a complete history of Australia.

We arrived into Darwin at 5am on 1st June somewhat tired, so to freshen up, the first activity Tourism Australia had organised for us was a swim in the Darwin Wave Lagoon where a palm-fringed swimming pool would at twenty minute intervals burst into ocean-like waves at the sound of a siren. That certainly woke me up.

As we had two days before the workshops started they had organised tours for us of Arnhem Land and Kakadu National Park. The stunning scenery of Kakadu was featured in the first *Crocodile Dundee* movie starring Paul Hogan. To describe it as spectacular would be like calling the Olympics a minor sporting event! Back in Darwin we went to the Mindil Beach Sunset Market. There was an open display from Territory Wildlife Adventure which specialised in snake handling. Now I'm pretty scared of snakes and they can be quite nasty, but way back in the early 70s, I did experience handling a python when we did a Radio Clyde Roadshow from Calderpark Zoo near Glasgow. I wanted our presenter to handle the snake but he refused till I showed him how easy it was. I would never ask someone to do something I was not prepared to try, though I may have had to take a change of underwear after that one. I did it, but inwardly I was scared shitless!

At Mindil Beach the two handlers were very informative about snakes which are not normally aggressive unless you stand on them or invade their territory. They are delicate and temperamental – just like a woman I thought then, but this is not acceptable these days even to think it! The handlers told the tale of the rainbow serpent snake which was the key to the Aboriginal Dreamtime stories of creation. The most stunning display was when one of the handlers took a snake – a small python, I think, and wrapped it round the body of a female onlooker. He then proceeded to place the snake's head in his mouth! It was probably not to everyone's taste but the snake seemed happy. Don't try this at home! He also warned us just how dangerous crocodiles could be. You can't outrun them. They can swim at around a speed of 18km per hour while you can usually just manage 2km per hour. They don't have great eyesight but sense your presence by hearing or vibration. Never risk a swim in a peaceful billabong (isolated pond in the outback) as crocs will be lurking. In the height of the wet season in January there is severe flooding and in some areas crocs will make their way into towns and swim along the main street!

After the workshops the group I was in was led by Tourism Australia's Glen Davis. He happened at that time to be their UK based trainer for the travel trade and we were already great friends. I'll digress briefly to tell how one night back in Glasgow a year earlier at the appropriate venue of the Walkabout Bar, I had become exceedingly drunk in his company and was telling things to him from my past that certainly will not appear in this book (sorry to disappoint). At one point in the evening I nipped outside for a smoke but when I tried to re-enter, the security staff would not let me back in as they said I was too drunk. Surprisingly I am quite a quiet rational person when pissed, so I agreed with them and didn't argue! They then reconsidered and reckoned if I knew I was drunk I would not be in any danger so they allowed me back in to say goodbye to him and pick up my stuff! So, back to the trip.

On June 6th we headed to Adelaide for a five day trip around the Barossa Valley. We had two nights in Adelaide first and onwards to the vineyards. It was a wine-lovers trip visiting such wineries as Jacob's Creek, The Louise and Wolf Blass. While I am not a great wine lover due to a bad teenage experience with Lutomer Riesling, a Slovenian sweet white wine, I would enjoy the occasional taste but at least the food was outstanding at all the restaurants. Australians have wonderful names for their eateries like the Hog's Breath Cafe or the Duck's Nuts Bar & Grill and slogans like "enlightenment through beer"!

I like to think of myself a being rather quirky – just weird enough to be interesting and intriguing, but not enough to repel. So when a couple of quirky hotels came up on our itinerary I was certainly intrigued. The first was in the town of Melrose which is around 175 miles north of Adelaide on the way into the Flinders Ranges National Park. The North Star Hotel has four rooms, a cottage and two outdoor trucks converted to rooms – Red and Green. The Red Truck has one queen bed, the Green Truck has one queen and a sofa bed and both have ensuite bathrooms.

They have a sister quirky hotel which just happened by a quirk of fate, or perhaps good planning, to be our next stop, Parachilna. The Prairie Hotel was built to serve the railway line that runs between Port Augusta and Leigh Creek that at one time connected passenger traffic with the old Ghan line to Alice Springs. In its restaurant the hotel serves feral animals like camel, goat and pig as well as kangaroo and emu. I enjoyed a bit of camel and happy to say it didn't give me the hump. The hotel is the only building remaining of the old railway town and the resident population is said to be just two! But they do have an airstrip just in case the Flying Doctor is needed.

Nearing the end of my Australian adventure we headed to the luxury eco resort Rawnsley Park Station in what was probably the most peaceful place at which I have ever stayed. It has a Homestead which is three kilometres from the main reception, with a private pool, two bedrooms with separate bathrooms and an outdoor shower. No need for curtains as there are no other humans around for miles, though you may have a few sheep staring at you. After such a hectic trip it was so relaxing and peaceful. At night the air was clear, the sky bright and the emotion heavenly. Just in case you fancy it, solitude comes at a price of 610 Australian Dollars for a night. The next day it was homeward from Adelaide to Singapore and on to London with Qantas.

Now Corroboree for UK travel agents happens every couple of years. Companies sending agents to the event have to pay a fee which goes towards the airfare and organisation. The exhibitors at the workshops also have to pay substantial sums to take part. When the 2013 event came round it was to be held in Cairns but I knew that there was little chance Travel 2 would send me as there were many more Australian specialists in the company who had not yet been. As I'd found the workshops so valuable, I contacted Glen Davis from Tourism Australia to see if there was any way he could get me accreditation to attend the workshops without actually signing up for the whole thing. I would pay for my flights and accommodation myself and it would be part of a big trip I was planning to include New Zealand and Thailand. Glen came up trumps for me. Not only did I get special accreditation but he also put me on one of the familiarisation trips to explore Port Douglas and Daintree. On the 10th of May 2013 I flew out from Glasgow with Emirates who were by that time my airline of choice to Australia. I first headed to Auckland via Dubai and Melbourne where I stayed two nights before flying back to Cairns via Sydney arriving on 16th May.

I did the usual round of workshops explaining to exhibitors that they were so good the last time I had to come back for more. As was their style, Tourism Australia had provided stunning evening entertainments the best of which was provided at the Tjabukai Aboriginal Cultural Park. They claimed to have a rather big backyard which stretched all the way to Perth in Western Australia, a mere 2,780 miles away. Dinner snacks ranged from crocodile with rice noodles to mini kangaroo burgers with mango chutney. Glen had also fixed some excursions for me including a trip on the Skyrail Rainforest Cableway which takes you over the Barron Gorge and up to Kuranda. Not having a great affinity for heights I avoided the glass-bottomed cable cars for fear of leaving a brown stain on the floor.

On a trip to Mossman Gorge in the Daintree Rainforest I learned how to make shampoo out of tree leaves from our Aboriginal guide as well as some fascinating info about the wildlife. In the daytime big pythons stay up in treetops to catch the sun, and they come down at night to kill their prey either by asphyxiation or strangulation. Then there are the rather large flightless birds, the cassowaries. The females are 2 metres high while the male is just 1.4 metres. She weighs about 90 kilos while he is a measly 50. The females prefer several partners and will play the field for suitable suitors. Once she lays her eggs, she walks away from them and one of the males will claim those eggs and for 50 days incubate them. Once the chicks hatch the males will raise the kids for two years until they can survive on their own. It's certainly a good life for the girls! But don't mess with any of them as they can turn nasty if threatened and attack you with their vicious claws.

Other ways of getting attacked by vicious animals would be to annoy a crocodile in the Daintree River where they are among the largest in the world. Genuine crocodile skin handbags start at around $1,000 while a shoulder bag from Gucci could come in around $25,000. Personally I would leave those crocs alone.

When Corroberee 2015 came around I had planned to repeat my 2013 trip by paying for my flights and sorting out accommodation myself, but Travel 2 said they could not give me the time off as there would not be enough Australian Specialists left in Glasgow to attend to our customers. Then one of the consultants who had been selected had to drop out and I was to go in their place!

The flights were to be with Singapore Airlines whom I loved based on my First Class trip from Bangkok to San Francisco in July 1997, however my experiences on this excursion did not start well. We were scheduled to take the train from Glasgow to Manchester on 23rd April to catch our flight the following morning but there was major disruption on the West Coast Main Line with no trains operating. The organisation around the replacement bus services was chaotic. Our group was split up and we boarded separate buses to take us as far as Carlisle to change to an onward coach service to Preston where we managed to catch a train to Manchester. We made our hotel near the airport around midnight.

All our flights were to be in Economy Class which, on reflection, was fair enough as the majority of the customers we booked would travel that way. At this point in my life I had been spoilt by too many long trips in Business Class so it was a bit of a culture shock for me. The flight had a touchdown in Munich and for some crazy reason we all had to get off the aircraft. The total journey time was over 20 hours so when we arrived in Singapore at 7.00 am the next day I was pretty shattered. Our onward flight to Australia was not till 9.00 pm and it was to Melbourne where we would connect with a Virgin Australia flight to our final destination of Adelaide. This was frustrating as Singapore Airlines actually had a direct flight between Singapore and Adelaide. I would never have recommended any of our customers to do this. Perhaps the direct flight was full.

With fourteen hours to spend in Singapore you would have thought that we would have had a chance to freshen up and at least have a shower. Instead, a full day of activities had been organised for us. It started with a tour of the airport then at 10 am we boarded a bus which was to be our base for the next eight hours as we explored the city where we sampled its delights. At one point the tiredness was so overwhelming that we considered bribing the bus driver to take us back to the airport! We were finally dropped off at 6.00 pm. I was lucky at that point as I was able to access the Singapore Airlines Star Alliance Lounge for a shower due to my Million Mile Status.

My hotel in Adelaide made up for all the discomforts and disruptions on the trip to Australia. The InterContinental was in the heart of the city, next door to the Convention Centre and to my delight it was close to the Sky City Casino! I fancied a go at a pokie. Now before you think this is some form of sexual deviancy, a "pokie" is the Australian term for a slot machine or as they are sometimes affectionately known in the UK, a one-armed bandit. The term "pokie" is from the time when video poker machines were in pubs and clubs in Australia. Video Poker seems to have died out in favour of gaming machines using video displays to simulate physical reels. On my first night at the casino I was $700 up! How I loved Adelaide and how stupid I was not to follow my own rules of gambling as over the next two nights I proceeded to put it all back in!

The workshops for Corroboree over the three day period were in the same format as previous events. I renewed friendships with many of the suppliers and delighted them when appropriate by showing them how their products were displayed in our Travel 2 Australia brochure. The evening social parties had style especially one which had been marked on our itinerary as TBA. At the final session of the last training day we were asked to look underneath our chairs for an envelope. In it was an invite to be served dinner at Parklands Terminal by the catering crew of the luxury train *The Ghan* and check out the train itself which I had travelled on the previous year from Darwin to Adelaide.

As I'd been a last-minute substitute on this trip, I had not been able to pick the area for the familiarisation part of the trip, but was delighted to be returning to Cairns and Port Douglas for another Reef and Rainforest experience. For some of this I was covering old ground like Tjabukai Aboriginal Experience and the Skyrail with the Kuranda Scenic Railway but added to those attractions was a trip to Hartley's Crocodile Adventure where I could pet a koala, jump in cage with a crocodile or take a duck tour through the rainforest. I thought at one point I was going to be shark bait when I took a trip on *Sailaway* out to the Great Barrier Reef and went snorkelling to explore the reef. I love swimming and can actually open my eyes underwater but this time I used the goggles. I caught my knee on a bit of coral and blood started to seep out. I had it in my head that sharks can smell blood up to three miles away – well according to National Geographic that is one of the talents of the Great White Shark. I headed straight back to the boat where first aid was applied and tiny bits of living coral removed from my leg. I also felt a sense of shame for doing damage to the world's ecosystem but at least I hadn't been part of a crocodile sandwich!

This was my last Corroboree trip. I now wanted to be in control of where I went and what I saw in Australia and also which airlines I flew with. My future trips would involve destinations that I had yet to explore – places like Brisbane, Kangaroo Island, Ayers Rock (Uluru), Tasmania and Hamilton Island.

I made a total of 26 trips to Australia and were I to list them all in detail you would probably suffer jet lag just reading the itineraries. I used a variety of routings and shared most of my business between two airlines, Emirates and United who were actually deadly rivals. This may seem odd as there was little overlap in their routes but United along with Delta and American tried to claim that Emirates and other Gulf airlines received unfair subsidies from their governments. This was proved not to be the case but it didn't stop these airlines trying to whip up political support. In my view were Emirates and United to work in partnership it could be an unbeatable combination.

My flights with Emirates did not start until October 2005 when I did a quick trip out to Thailand from Glasgow via Dubai and was lucky enough to be upgraded on the Glasgow sectors. My next Emirates trip was not till June 2009 which also happened to be my first trip to Australia but just to Sydney and again I had the benefits of a few sector upgrades which gave me a taste for the comforts of their Business Class. It wasn't till November 2012 when I was given Gold status in their Skywards frequent flyer programme for a major trip that took in Bangkok in Thailand, Melbourne in Australia and both North and South Islands in New Zealand that I was really hooked. The Gold level of Skywards meant that I would have lounge access at all points on the itinerary. This was a major benefit because their lounges had amazing buffet service food and drinks as well as showers. I was pretty well covered on my trips anywhere in the world now for the joys of airline lounges as the combination of Star Alliance and Emirates made my long treks tolerable.

In Melbourne I found Elvis! It was down at St. Kilda in the delightful Claypots Seafood Bar where "Elvis" in the form of Rohan Hammet does his fun impersonation of The King with a three piece band in the rather small bar space. Yes, you could say I was All Shook Up!

Another discovery for me was the delightful Puffing Billy railway which runs from the suburb of Belgrave through the Dandenong Ranges to Gembrook. It's a heritage railway experience run by volunteers as well as some paid staff. Now, you'll not take the Puffing Billy for its speed as it moves so slowly you are quicker walking. The delight for me at that time is you could sit on the window ledges of the carriages with your legs dangling outside. Sad to say I believe that today this is no longer permitted due to Health & Safety concerns.

Puffing Billy, Melbourne

New Zealand was to be a very different set of train experiences and in my view the best way to see the magnificent scenery as I travelled on the three main tourist trips; *Northern Explorer* from Auckland to Wellington, *Coastal Pacific* from Picton to Christchurch and *TranzAlpine* from Christchurch to Greymouth and back. On the last one I made a video for YouTube and was really proud of my well edited and captioned product. That was until I checked other YouTube offerings on the same subject and was put to shame by the outstanding quality of one which was shot from the driver's cab giving the best possible views. My hopes of being another Ken Burns – ace documentary producer – were dashed!

New Zealand does have casinos and I was intrigued by the operation of the biggest one which was the Sky City in Auckland. At the time of my first visit they had a weird operational system for collecting your winnings which seemed to be run on civil service paperwork principles. If you won on a slot machine you would have to summon an attendant who would verify your win, then write out a voucher which you would then take over to the cashier's cage. One cashier would stamp your voucher and then send you to a second window where another cashier would issue the money. My winnings were small and it was a bit of a hassle. At least it was a lot better that my first experience in Macau back in 1993 when I had a reasonable win but I could only cash it out with the aid of a "fixer" who took 25%! Fortunately Macau casinos are now properly regulated and the fixers are no more.

To keep my status up in Emirates Skywards I resolved to use them where possible for my Australian trips but I also had a desire to keep the USA on my radar. I had a strange craving to fly over the North Pole not just to see if, to quote Chico Marx, "there ain't no sanity clause", but just for the experience. Emirates flights to the West coast USA take the Polar route so I started hunting through the reservations systems to find the best Business Class fares because for such a long flight from Dubai there was no way I would go in the back of the bus.

Inventory management is a very sophisticated system with airlines. Back in 1991, I had bought and studied what was then considered the bible of revenue management – *"Flying Off Course"* by Professor Rigas Doganis from the Cranfield Institute of Technology which helped me fathom out the crazy range of fares offered by airlines. A little sidetrack here about the name Doganis. In the early days of EasyJet, I interviewed the founder Stelios Haji-Ioannou for Radio Clyde in our Clydebank studios. Accompanying him was a TV crew from Channel 4 and the director was Dimitri Doganis. I mentioned to him that he had an unusual surname and that the only other Doganis I knew of was Rigas. He responded with "That's my father!". While the interview recording was supposed to last five minutes we actually talked for half an hour! Once I get started on aviation it's like a runaway train. Sad to say I don't know if my contribution even made the final cut.

It's time to polarise things. I studied the various business class fares offered by Emirates and noted that while the Dubai to the west coast of the USA were pretty expensive, you would sometimes find special promotional fares from other countries but going via Dubai that were considerably cheaper even though you routed through Dubai. It would depend on the season and availability was usually quite tight. Now this might seem illogical as you were going to have an extra flight just to get to Dubai but it was all down to competitive fares from other airlines in the marketplace between the point of origin and destination. Between 2014 and 2018 I found three starting points at various times that offered these special fares. They were Bangkok (BKK), Ho Chi Minh City (SGN) and Cape Town (CPT). To get the fare you had to purchase a round trip ticket and the penalties for changes and cancellations were quite severe. I would buy a separate ticket to get me from Glasgow to the point of origin on the transatlantic trip. This was usually part of a larger itinerary and all I would be doing was breaking my journey to take a wee side trip to the USA!

To price everything on one single ticket originating in Glasgow would have been outrageous costing around £8,000 more!

It was a rather special occasion for my first Polar expedition on 10th April 2014. To mark the 10th Anniversary of service to Glasgow, Emirates operated as a one-off the Airbus 380, so I splashed out on a First Class ticket routing through Dubai and Hong Kong and on to Bangkok. In Thailand my separate ticket kicked in and, sad to say, I was slumming it in Business Class for the transatlantic flights. For this mega trip I had chosen BKK in Thailand and flew to Los Angeles where I picked up a round trip on a separate ticket to Las Vegas and it all went to plan. This was to be the pattern for future trips but not without some nasty problems. My one disappointment on this trip was when the moving map showed our position to be above the North Pole, I looked out the window and all I could see was a complete whiteout!

My second Polar trip was relatively simple and gave me my first experience of South Africa. I had won from

Travel 2 some accommodation nights in Cape Town, Stellenbosch and Robertson. I had to book my own flights and sort out transfers between each hotel. Emirates would kindly provide the chauffer–drive to and from the airport. I decided to tack on another side trip to the USA. On 24th May 2015 I flew from Glasgow via Dubai to Cape Town, stayed eight nights then on to Los Angeles for my usual United flights across to Vegas for a week and back to Cape Town. To prepare me for the trip my light reading for the flight was Nelson Mandela's *Long Walk to Freedom*. My only disappointment on the trip was bad weather did not permit a trip to Robben Island where Mandela had been imprisoned.

When I reached Los Angeles I managed I quick visit to see Ross King MBE, former Saturday Boy at Radio Clyde and now Emmy winner at his amazing Hollywood home overlooking that famous Hollywood sign. I was happy he did not throw me into his swimming pool!

On 2nd October 2015 I flew out to Bangkok with Emirates for my third Polar excursion then on to Vietnam. Now Ho Chi Minh City, or as everyone still calls it, Saigon, presented a minor issue due to visa requirements for Vietnam. At that time you were only permitted one visa-free entry to the country but my trips would require two, unless I was just transiting the airport on one of the trips. This could be risky for the transit trips. I would be using two different airlines and so the connections would not be protected! To reach Saigon on 5th October I used Vietnam Airlines on a flight that arrived at 2120 leaving me three hours for my onward flight with Emirates. I had to stay airside and wait an hour for the transfer desk to open up. The desk was operated on behalf of Emirates by SAGS – Saigon Ground

Services and a delightful agent Miss Th Phuong Hong arrived to check me in for my flight to Dubai and onto Los Angeles. Disaster! It appeared that my ESTA – Visa Waiver for the USA was not valid! Prior to the trip I had secured, I thought, my ESTA a month in advance but I had placed one digit wrong for my passport number and as it did not match so I would be denied boarding! She was an angel because she let me use her terminal to re-apply for the ESTA and after about 20 minutes it came back approved! At that time you could get instant approval. I was relieved and delighted so I wrote to Emirates and to SAGS to say what excellent service I had received.

Six months later I repeated the trip Vietnam via Australia but this time going to Los Angeles for Las Vegas. When I arrived in Saigon my angel from SAGS met me off the flight and escorted me to my Emirates connection. My letters of praise had done the job and both Emirates and SAGS had complimented her on her outstanding service.

I had two more Polar trips in June 2017 and April 2018 both using Bangkok as my ticketing point.

For the first of them I had set up my usual convoluted routing with several objectives in mind. On the 14th June I flew from Glasgow via Dubai to Melbourne where I indulged in a dose of "Elvis" at Claypots in St. Kilda. On Sunday 18th it was off to Ayers Rock (Uluru) for an experience that would be weird and wonderful – a sunset camel ride. When I arrived at Uluru Camel Tours I imagined all the camels were eyeing up the visitors and thinking to themselves "I hope I don't get an ugly one!" The camel attendants had lined up a train of around twenty of these delightful ships of the desert and after instructing us on the art of sitting safely on the hump, they assisted us in mounting our camels. Each camel had its own name and while they all looked the same to me the camel attendants seemed to easily identify them. Normally they would load two riders on to each beast but occasionally there would be just one. Now I'm not sure whether it was my size or my personality but I was given a camel to myself. His name was Darcy and we got along just fine.

The sunset was stunning, the sky cloud patterns were intoxicating, and after two hours on Darcy's hump my groin was aching. The next day I was scheduled to fly in the afternoon from Ayers Rock to Sydney when the curse of Uluru struck – it's a kind of Ozzie Murphy's Law. There was a technical problem with the aircraft and the nearest engineer was three hours away by road in Alice Springs. I started planning alternate arrangements but there were no other flights to get me to Sydney. One of my delightful colleagues back at Travel 2 suggested I hired a camel and rode the 1,355 miles to Sydney, probably not an option unless it was jet powered! Fortunately the engineer managed to get a lift in a light aircraft from Alice Springs, fixed the problem and we were on our way just three hours late. I had a couple of nights at the Four Seasons hotel in Sydney before heading to Bangkok arriving at 4pm.

My onward flight via Dubai to the USA was not till 1.35 am so I had around 9 hours to kill after I picked up my boarding passes for the transatlantic flights so it was off to the Emirates lounge for some food and a freshen up shower. Around midnight we started to board the Airbus A380 where the Business Class cabin is located on the upper deck. As I took my seat the crew were dealing with five male passengers who were rather rowdy and had brought their own alcohol on board and were helping themselves to it. It is a strict rule that any alcohol brought on board must be served to the passengers by the cabin crew to ensure the safety of the flight is not endangered by any of them becoming drunk and incapable. The five miscreants then tried to order more drinks from the flight attendants and continued to annoy the other passengers. The captain took the decision that all five should be offloaded. What was outstanding was the discreet manner in which the crew handled the situation by soft words and gentle persuasion. It was product of excellent training that the offenders were removed and their bags offloaded without the aid of law enforcement. The crew asked me to help them with a witness report which I gladly provided. We were an hour late but I made the connection OK in Dubai and my flight on to San Francisco was only spoilt by a screaming child who managed to keep it up for almost the entire 16 hour flight. I do wish airlines would give us a child-free cabin for such long flights.

At San Francisco I sailed through immigration thanks to my Global Entry status and made it to Circus Circus in time for the Summer Splash Slot Tournament. These tournaments are fun but once again my score was pretty low. I did get lucky on my favourite slot machine "Aces & Eights" with a wee win of just over $2,000. My good friend from Tourism Australia, Glen Davis, had just taken up a new job based in Los Angeles looking after incentive marketing to Oz, so I arranged to pop in and see him while I transited LA on my way back to Dubai.

I took an early morning United flight from Las Vegas which would give me plenty of time before my Emirates onwards flight to Dubai at 4.40 pm. Glen had suggested to me that I take an Uber from Los Angeles Airport (LAX) to his office at Century City but I had a strong distrust of ride-sharing services, preferring the traditional taxis. So I went to the taxi rank at the airport and got a properly licensed cab within five minutes. My driver, Artur from Armenia, was delightful. He actually had an Uber pricing app on his phone and he showed me how much more Uber could hit you for compared to a regular taxi. We got on so well that I took his number and arranged to text him when I was ready to return to the airport even though he said it could be up to half an hour wait depending where he was. I did just that and also noted that I could book him in advance the next time I needed a taxi at LAX. The return home journey with Emirates was uneventful but when I got back into the office on 2nd July I was hit with my desk decorated for my 70th Birthday!

The second trip was almost a disaster thanks to United cancelling my flight from Vegas to Los Angeles on 15th April 2018. The trip had not started well. I had planned on flying from Glasgow via Dubai to Perth for one night then on to Sydney. The departure from Glasgow was substantially delayed while they offloaded a passenger who had taken ill. When we got to Dubai very late the flight to Perth had closed but I was met at the gate by an Emirates agent who advised that they had rebooked me on to a direct flight to Sydney which was just about to depart! They had assumed that Sydney was my final destination as my "connection" in Perth was under 24 hours. I made it OK but lost out on a night at the Crown Casino in Perth! I made it to Vietnam and on to the USA without further incident.

The tournament at Circus Circus was on a pirate theme so I decided to buy myself a pirate outfit to enter into the spirit of things. I managed to acquire several of what I hoped would be temporary tattoos on my face, arms and hands. I am not an aficionado of the Polynesian practice of inserting ink, dyes or pigments into the skin. For some it may be a manly turn on, but for me it is not my scene. Fortunately after a few days the temporary transfers wore off as I didn't think that the skull and crossbones on my cheeks would help at immigration counters around the world.

It was when I tried to leave Las Vegas that disaster struck. I had booked into First Class with United for a flight that was due to depart at 1040 am arriving into Los Angeles at 1205. This would have given me plenty of time to catch my Emirates flight at 1640 to Dubai. I got an e-mail from United at 6.47 am to tell me my flight had been cancelled due to maintenance but they had rebooked me on to the next available flight which unfortunately would have arrived after my Emirates flight had departed! It was time to panic – well not really because I perversely enjoy challenges like this. I quickly searched for alternate direct flights from Vegas to Los Angeles but found that everything was full! I had to get to the airport fast so with a speedy checkout from Circus Circus at 7am, I grabbed a cab to the airport. The driver asked me "which terminal"? And I responded "I don't know yet!" While on the way to the airport I had managed to find on my iPhone an indirect service going Las Vegas via Phoenix which would get me in to Los Angeles at 12 noon with Southwest Airlines. The only snag was the connection in Phoenix was just 45 minutes! I decided to risk it otherwise my only other choice was to grab a taxi to take me to LA! I booked the flights and just made it just in time for the short hop to Phoenix. I also made the connection in Phoenix with ease and was delighted to look out the window and watch my bag being loaded onto the connecting flight!

In November 2014, I discovered a great fare offered by United for flights between Australia (Sydney, Melbourne or Brisbane) and Las Vegas of just £600 round trip. What was so good about this was enhanced by my Star Alliance Million Miler status which meant on an Economy Class fare I would automatically be seated in the Economy Plus section of the aircraft which just happened to be on the Trans-Pacific sectors the Boeing 787 Dreamliner. This became a template for seven further trips but a couple had disastrous consequences.

The first trip on this kind of routing was on 8th November 2014 when I flew out with Emirates via Dubai to Perth, Western Australia where I spent a couple of nights with time for a visit to my favourite bar "The Lucky Shag". I wasn't lucky but I did love the names Australians give some of their bars. On the same theme there once was a "Fanny's Tavern" in Newcastle, New South Wales or there's the Humpty Doo Hotel in Northern Territory. Now before you get the wrong idea about "The Lucky Shag" the shag is actually a variety of cormorant and when they were looking for a name for the bar, a shag was seen rising from the sea with two fish in its mouth and the name came up as the lucky shag.

I flew on to Darwin for one night then picked up the luxury train, *The Ghan*, for a three day trip for the 1,900 miles to Adelaide. Now at that time there was no Wi-Fi on board and as you travelled through the outback there was little phone reception. In your cabin you did have a TV screen which gave information about your journey. What

I thought would have been really stunning was to have a camera mounted in the cab of the locomotive giving the driver's eye view of the track ahead. I was told that this was not technically possible as the locomotives were owned by a different company. At Alice Springs we had time for a tour of the town and in particular the Royal Flying Doctor Service Museum. I saw enough to resolve to return to this interesting oasis in the outback at some point. From Adelaide I caught a Qantas flight to Melbourne and then it was the Dreamliner flight with United to Los Angeles for Las Vegas and back to Melbourne. I managed to have three nights in Thailand before heading home.

The second trip started off smoothly enough when on 30th September 2016 I flew Emirates out to Sydney via Dubai and Perth with a side trip to Port Douglas. On 10th October United took me on the Dreamliner from Melbourne to Los Angeles (LAX) and on to Las Vegas. United Airlines occupies Terminals 7 and 8 at LAX. These were undergoing a massive redevelopment programme which had reduced the number of gates available for United to operate from. Now logically you would think United would have thinned out their flight schedule to match the number of gates available. Here's how it went horribly wrong and how United were economical with the truth when it happened. I was scheduled on a United flight due to depart from Vegas at 1910 and arrive into Los Angeles at 2029 in plenty of time for my onward connection to Sydney at 2250.

Here's the full story of what actually happened. The flight from Vegas at 1906 took an 80 minute "Air Traffic Control (ATC) delay". I didn't quite understand this as weather at LAX was fine and no other airlines were being held up by an "ATC delay". The aircraft was ready for boarding on time but this was delayed slightly. We pushed back around 30 mins late then we were then held a further 40 mins before we took off. The Captain advised us this was an "ATC delay".

We eventually touched down at LAX at 2145 then waited an hour on the taxiway for a gate to be free at the United Terminal. I rushed to Gate 74 where UA 839 to Sydney was still on the stand but there were no staff in the vicinity of the gate area and all the doors to the jetway were closed. As a result I missed the flight. There was a line of over twenty people at the Customer Service desk and only one agent looking after all the misconnects. Fortunately UA found more staff but even then it was over an hour before I could be attended to. While standing in line for the Customer Service agent I checked on my phone at United.com to see how I had been protected due to the misconnection. I was horrified to see their system had booked me on to San Francisco on the Monday evening 17th then on from SFO to SYD on the Tuesday evening 18th which would have meant that I would now arrive in Sydney two days later than planned. This was totally unacceptable especially for a Star Alliance Lifetime Gold Million Miler.

So I called the Premier Priority Desk on my mobile and got a helpful agent who understood the situation and instead of making me wait 2 days put me on the Qantas flight at 2230 on Monday night from LAX direct to SYD arriving Wednesday morning at 0730. This was not normal as Qantas and United were not partners in any way however it is more in recognition of my frequent flyer status that they had done this. So when I eventually reached the Customer Service desk – I got another helpful

United agent – I took her name Linda Wilson – and she called up the my reservation and could see what had been done to rebook me. After a bit of discussion, she issued me with hotel vouchers for the Residence Inn at the airport and meal vouchers to cover my needs till my flight the next night.

She "booked " me in to the Residence Inn LAX and issued me with two x 1 night stay vouchers as I would need to keep the room till around 7 pm and also 3 x $10 meal vouchers. I took the shuttle to the Residence Inn arriving at around 2 am where the Duty Manager told me the Residence Inn could not accept the United vouchers as their systems had all gone down and I would have to go back to the airport and get United to issue vouchers for another hotel! He did not seem in any way interested in trying to help me.

By the time I got back to the airport there were no United staff left, and the terminal was full of workers doing the renovations. I spotted three United staff that had been working the Customer Service desk but were now making their way home. I asked them for help and one of them tried to log on to a United Terminal but discovered that all the power was now out throughout the terminal due to the ongoing reconstruction work. She advised me to go to any hotel on the first hotel available hotel shuttle and send the bill to United. The first shuttle to arrive was for the Hilton where I received excellent service at check in and they could let me keep the room for late check out.

On arrival in Sydney I had been booked separately with Virgin Australia to fly on to Ayers Rock (Uluru) and spend one night at the Desert Gardens Hotel with the *Sounds of Silence Dinner* package before flying back to Sydney for a further three night stay. I had to cancel all this which regrettably was non-refundable but I was able to claim it back on my travel insurance. Had United been less ambitious in trying to squeeze too many flights into their limited number of gates at LAX, none of this would have happened. I did receive a $400 voucher from United for the inconvenience and in retrospect the fact that they booked me on to Qantas at what must have been at considerable cost did them credit. Ayers Rock could wait. I was sure it would still be there on my next trip.

Bryce Canyon USA

In October 2017 I flew out once again from Glasgow with Emirates this time going via Dubai, Kuala Lumpur, Singapore and Melbourne before taking United to Las Vegas via Los Angeles. It was another tournament at Circus Circus on an Oktoberfest theme and Magi Sloan had come out from Glasgow to join me and beat me in the tournament! As I had a full week there I took in several sightseeing trips and shows and met up with my colleague from my 3C days, Pat Geary. One of the trips I took with *Detours of Nevada* was to the Skywalk at the Grand Canyon West. Be warned, you are not permitted to take cameras or phones on to the Skywalk. It is owned by the Hualapai Tribe who seem to be rather expert in making money out of the visiting tourists.

John with Ronnie Bergman (left) Washington DC

To avoid the danger of repeating my nightmare experience at Los Angeles airport I sensibly decided to route via San Francisco on my way back to Australia arriving in Sydney on 20th October where I met up with my good friend from Radio Clyde days, Ronnie Bergman, who was on his own mega excursion around Australia. I then was able to do my trip to Ayers Rock (Uluru) where I went for another camel ride. I had hoped to be reunited with my pet camel Darcy but it was his day off. I think he had heard I was coming and didn't fancy my fat ugliness on his back again! It was then upwards and onwards to Alice Springs by bus where I stayed two nights. The highlight for me was the Overlanders Steakhouse (now sadly closed) where the signature item was the "Drovers Blowout" which had tastings of camel, crocodile, emu and kangaroo. They had a lovely touch that when you checked in for your table, they would first find out where you were from then put a little flag from your country onto your table. Yes, they had a Scottish Flag!

From Alice Springs I flew to Adelaide to catch the *Indian Pacific* to Perth. In Perth I checked in to the Crowne Plaza. Naturally I had been enjoying the fun of various casinos on this trip but by the time I hit Perth my funds were somewhat depleted. However the Crown Casino was just a short walk away so on my last night in Australia, I popped in for a wee play on the pokies. Now this casino is partnered with the Crown in Melbourne so my player's card would work there. I was doing OK but getting a bit tired and was about to pack it in when I looked at how much I had racked up on my players card. A few dollars play more would help my status. Wham! I won a major jackpot of several thousand Australian Dollars. I cashed in immediately and returned

Camel Ride at Uluru Australia

to my hotel with a minor problem to consider. While I'd bought all my currency on a "buy back" deal where they will give you the same rate of exchange that they used for your purchase for any money you have left, you'll not get that same rate for any amounts over what you purchased. I then had a brilliant idea. I would change at Perth Airport the surplus Australian Dollars into US Dollars. When I returned to Glasgow the currency exchange bought back ALL the currency they had sold me! I was lucky as the amount was not over $10,000 otherwise I would have had a lot of form filling for customs. Every country has limits on the total amount of cash in any currency that you are carrying without having to declare it – even in transit. If you don't declare it they can confiscate it!

On my next Emirates/United combination I did something that I hadn't done for over ten years! On 11th

Indian Pacific Australia

October 2018, I flew out via Dubai and Bangkok to Sydney where I then proceeded to Hamilton Island then down to Hobart, Tasmania. While I was in Australia there was a wee bit of a Royal run around when a young couple called, I believe, Harry and Meghan, were doing their bit for a former colony. On 18th October I flew on United's Dreamliner to San Francisco and on to Las Vegas. At McCarran Airport I picked up a car from Alamo. Nothing unusual about that you might think except that I hadn't driven for almost eleven years! Technology had moved on so much that I couldn't figure out how to start the car without help from the agent. I was used to putting a key into the ignition, making sure it wasn't in gear, and turning the key to start the engine. Now it is all sophisticated and electronic. I spent 15 minutes familiarising myself with the controls and then drove out of the depot towards Circus Circus via the freeway. By the time I reached the hotel I was asking myself why I hadn't driven for so long because I thoroughly enjoyed it. I find driving in the USA a real pleasure. Just keep checking your mirrors watching for blind spots and signal your intentions before changing lanes. I invited my good friend Dana Pitcher who was a slot manager at Circus Circus to come with me for a drive out of town so she could criticise my driving techniques. The biggest compliment she paid me was in telling me at the end of the trip that at no time was she instinctively looking for the brake pedal! A car would be a must for me on future trips.

Three more trips followed on a similar pattern in March, May and October, 2019 with one major difference. On the March and May trips I decided to treat myself to United's Polaris Business Class on the flights from Los Angeles to

Melbourne, one using my United miles to upgrade and the other on a special cash offer from United which I couldn't resist. Now I'm a sucker for airline lounges especially those operated by Emirates which I consider to be among the best in the world but now they had serious competition from United. For those lucky sods travelling with United in the Polaris Business Class they had, at select locations, dedicated lounges which were only available to travellers in Polaris Class. Star Alliance card holders that had lounge access included would not be permitted in the Polaris Lounge unless of course if they had the appropriate ticket for their flight. The Polaris Lounge had everything you would want from an international buffet style dining to an a la carte restaurant. What I really appreciated was at every seat in the lounge there was a charging point for your portable electronic equipment. On the second trip I made sure I arrived real early so I could pig out on all the amazing food offerings. On that trip I had also decided to hire my car from Los Angeles to drive to Vegas and back. This enabled me to spend one night in Palm Springs on the way back and check out a couple of motels in Pasadena, LA County. You might wonder why Pasadena? To me it was the best base if you wanted to explore the greater Los Angeles area but I wanted to check the motels were not undesirable and my theories of accessibility were correct. In my very early visits to Los Angeles I had come across some real undesirable motels. In one, to put it crudely, the chalk marks outlining where the body had lain at a crime scene were still visible!

For my final trip in October 2019 on this combined airlines routing I tried desperately to get Polaris Class on my flight from Los Angeles but they were looking for something in the region of $7,000 for the flight so I resigned myself to the comfort of Economy Plus without the magic Polaris Lounge.

On my many trips to the USA I had noticed a customs and immigration facility called Global Entry so early in 2016 I made enquiries to see if I could qualify. Around 25 years earlier I had an INSPASS – INS Passenger Accelerated Service System which allowed me to enter the USA via an automated kiosk and really helped speed up the immigration process at certain airports. Unfortunately after 9/11 the system was discontinued. It was replaced by Global Entry but for quite a while this was only available to US citizens. Eventually UK citizens could apply for it but they had first to provide a background check from the UK government. This cost me £45 to obtain after which I had to apply to the US Customs and Border Protection (CBP) with a fee of $100 and the requirement to attend an interview at one of their offices. I chose Las Vegas for the interview so on March 17th, 2016 I had a 1pm appointment at their office at Terminal 3, McCarran Airport.

I was not sure of the exact location of their office so a couple of hours before my appointed time I ventured out to check the lie of the land. I arrived 90 minutes before my appointed time and went into the public area of the CBP office just in case they could take me earlier. The experience was quite daunting. There were several people waiting and a sign saying no service without an appointment! I observed the activity behind the counter and from the offices within. I found the demeanour of the officers attending to be quite intimidating and was not looking forward to my interview. Instead of hanging around I decided to return just a few minutes before my appointed time. When I came back I was disillusioned to see that several of the folk that had been waiting an hour before were still there. A few minutes later my name was called and I was led into a room to meet the CBP officer who would carry out the "interview". He was very pleasant, took my passport and driver's license to photocopy, asked me to provide fingerprints and took a digital biometric photograph. Then he told me I now have Global Entry for the next five years. I had expected a third-degree grilling but instead it was easy and he also handed me a comment card to send off about the quality of service I had received! The terms efficient and friendly are not often associated with US Government bureaucracy but in this case the service was outstanding.

I am a great fan of Facebook and I do not mind them targeting advertising based on what I like. I have nothing to fear except fear itself. I like to post all my travel plans on social media and do regular updates on my little excursions around the world. I pride myself in finding great value fares so when I posted on Facebook a trip I was planning in May 2016 to go out to Las Vegas from Glasgow via Belfast, New York, and Washington DC for a great round trip price of £572.60 I had a stalker! Ronnie Bergman used to work with me at Radio Clyde as a very able production assistant. He then went on to lecture in broadcasting at college and university. He had been following my Facebook itineraries and was inspired to do a similar trip to this one. Well, more than similar, an exact copy! He contacted me to say that he had tried to book the same itinerary on United's website but it was coming out over £3,000! Knowledge is power so I asked him how he had actually quoted the routing and apparently he had priced each sector separately instead of putting it all on the one ticket. What I had done was found an ex-Belfast fare with United that required special inventory classes and routings.

We worked together and soon had him sorted. I was very happy to have him for company on the trip and introduce him to the evils of the Ectoplasm themed slot tournament in Las Vegas. Not everything went quite to plan, though. First snag was in New York's Newark Airport where I had priority clearance with my Global Entry status and sped through immigration, customs and the security check for the connecting flight. Ronnie was not as lucky as he missed his connection and the next flight was not for another 3 hours. I checked in to our hotel at Washington Dulles then went back to meet Ronnie 3 hours later.

We had two amazing days exploring Washington DC with many remarkable photo opportunities. There were two that, for me, made the trip weird and wonderful. We came across a building that was the home to the Independent Order of Oddfellows and the plaque on the wall was screaming "selfie!" to us. Now this organisation is anything but weird and has the ethic of reciprocity – the principle of treating others as you would want to be treated. It is a non-political and non-sectarian fraternal order and it was the first fraternity in the United States to include both men and women back in 1851.

The wonderful part of the trip was the visit to the Smithsonian National Air and Space Museum but not the one in the National Mall in DC but the branch out near Dulles Airport at Chantilly, Virginia, known as the Steven V. Udvar-Hazy Center. On display were the Space Shuttle Discovery, a supersonic Concorde from Air France and the *Enola Gay*. This was the Boeing B17 Superfortress bomber

Enola Gay Smithsonian

which on 6th August, 1945, dropped the first atomic bomb on Hiroshima piloted by Colonel Paul Tibbets and curiously the aircraft was named after his mother, Enola Gay Tibbets.

After Washington we were scheduled to take an evening United flight from Dulles Airport to Las Vegas. I thought I should treat Ronnie to the United Lounge and had arranged a guest pass for him through their representative in Scotland, Tom Sneddon. That was fine for Ronnie, but I was denied access to the lounge! Call me Mr. Stupid, but I had forgotten that my access to United's lounges on my Million Miler status only applied on continuous journeys and as I had broken the trip for my than 24 hours they couldn't let me in! After that, all worked well for both of us in Las Vegas.

I had many other flights in the new millennium but most were without incident. I'd like to conclude this chapter with a story about an airport which struggled to get its customer priorities to my satisfaction when I was on a crazy day trip to Canada. It was on 31st August 2017 that Air Canada had organised for a small party from Travel 2 to take a day trip to Toronto leaving Glasgow at 0830 and arriving at 1030 at Pearson International Airport on their Air Canada Rouge service. We had a most excellent day which included lunch at the top of the CN Tower. The Air Canada Rouge service was split over a week between Glasgow and Edinburgh so for the return in the evening we flew overnight into Edinburgh Airport. We landed on time and as we disembarked we made our way along a corridor to International Arrivals when suddenly a door was closed in front of us stopping us in our tracks. The airport had started to board a British Airways domestic flight to London across our path. We were held standing in the corridor for fourteen minutes with no information while all the passenger for the BA flight were boarded! The issue at that time was the airport was undergoing reconstruction and had no means of providing separation of arriving and departing passengers without blocking this corridor. It would only have taken two minutes to clear all the arriving passengers from this corridor but I reckoned the airport must have thought that BA departures were more important than Air Canada arrivals. Or perhaps they were just not very well organised. Fortunately things at Edinburgh have improved and they now manage their passenger flows with far greater customer satisfaction.

Chapter 24

2020

Angel Number 2020.
Quarantined in Australia.
Escape home.

Opticians use the term 20/20 vision to describe normal eyesight. Spiritually, the Angel Number 2020 is telling you to be prepared for what is coming your way. Your guardian angels are telling you that changes are about to enter your life and you need to be prepared both mentally and physically! If I could only have seen what lay ahead at the start of 2020 then I might not have travelled.

January and February are peak months in the travel industry for bookings so I tended to work seven days a week and take time off later in the year for the extra days worked. So, my first trip was to be out on 13th March with Emirates from Glasgow via Dubai to Sydney. Then on 17th March taking United to Las Vegas via LAX and returning on 22nd March to Melbourne. I had planned a real treat to travel back from Melbourne on 28th March in First Class on Emirates via Dubai taking the Airbus A380 all the way to Glasgow as they were planning on operating that big bird into Scotland on a year round basis.

The Covid-19 outbreak was spreading quite rapidly at that time and I did consider cancelling the complete trip but then I decided to go ahead anyway. I would have a long layover of 18 hours in Dubai on the way out and while my bag would be checked straight though, I took a day room at the Ibis Deira. Between sleeps and eats I monitored what was happening in Australia and the USA. It looked like Donald Trump was going to include the UK in the travel ban to the USA so I started planning on staying in Australia and cancelling the side trip to America. The Australian border also looked like closing fast with the enforcement of self isolation for 14 days for all arrivals! I made it into Sydney with just 2 hours to spare before this requirement came in to effect. I was beginning to feel like Indiana Jones in *Raiders of the Lost Ark* where he is chased down a tunnel by a giant rolling ball!

I checked in to the Rydges at Sydney Airport for two nights on arrival on 15th March and proceeded to plan my alternate itinerary. I cancelled my United flights and they were good enough to allow me to use what I had paid towards any future flight with the airline within a year.

I formulated a basic plan to fly from Sydney to Cairns on 17th March and stay for three nights at the Hilton before moving on to Port Douglas to stay at The Meridian with my good friend John Haymes for a further four nights. Then I would fly on to Melbourne and staying five nights till it was time to catch my Emirates flights home. This may have looked like an excellent plan except for the Australian States planning on closing their individual borders and Emirates starting a wholesale cancellation of flights on their network. I booked my accommodation online for Cairns and Port Douglas. I already had Melbourne on my original itinerary so I kept the hotel booking at the CBD Hotel. For transfers in Cairns I usually use Exemplar and I thought, wrongly, that I could just book it on arrival at the airport. When I reached Cairns I found an Exemplar representative but he informed me that he couldn't take the booking and instead I had to go to the airport ground transportation desk. I didn't realise at the time that Exemplar could only pick up pre-booked hires and a rival company had the exclusive right to operate the desk. I booked all my transfers with them – airport to Hilton to Cairns and back to the airport. It turned out that they were unable to operate the last trip and passed the job on to Exemplar! They may be rivals but in that part of Queensland they all co-operate.

Cairns was curious. Social distancing measures were being introduced throughout the resort. Naturally I visited the Reef Casino over the three days and watched them gradually limit the number of customers, switch off every second pokie for social distancing, and close the restaurant.

On the second day I decided to go back up to Kuranda on the Scenic Railway. The train was almost empty! I had a few hours to explore the village and take a trip on the Kuranda Riverboat Cruise and feed some turtles.

On Friday 20th March I made it up to Port Douglas and checked in to the Meridian. I had considered taking some toilet rolls up to John Haymes as loo paper had been the subject of panic buying in Australia but instead a small quantity of Scotch whisky was in order.

On the Sunday the news came through that Emirates was suspending most flights from 29th March. At this point it looked like I would be OK as I would be on the final flight from Melbourne. I was beginning to get visions of the last chopper out of Saigon! Then Emirates announced it was suspending operations with almost immediate effect! I decided that I should go to Melbourne as planned and then try to work out how to get home. I could be stranded in Australia indefinitely! I may have to buy a one-way ticket on an airline that was still providing service to the UK or my best hope would be to see if I could switch my Emirates ticket to their partner airline Qantas. I kept chasing possibilities that all but one became impossibilities!

On 23rd March once again I made the last flight before the borders closed from Cairns down to Melbourne and checked in to the CBD Hotel (formerly Ibis) on Little Bourke Street. Melbourne was in lockdown and you were only permitted out for food and exercise. The restaurant was closed but they gave me five breakfast boxes for the duration of my stay. For other meals I had to go out for takeaway services which were all pretty reasonable especially the Korean barbecue special which I considered to be the dog's bollocks!

I spent a lot of time trying to find a chemist with stocks of hand sanitizer and managed a trip down to St Kilda on the 96 tram to visit my friends Noel and Brenda. Throughout the trip I had been ultra-cautious with any kind of contact and would even use a sanitized cloth on door handles. All the cafes and restaurants were closed and Elvis was in isolation somewhere so I couldn't pop into Claypots for his usual Saturday show. The biggest hardship for me was the fact that the Crown Casino was completely closed. I should have been happy at the money I had saved but couldn't help thinking about the poor starving pokies in the casino that were not being fed my dollars!

After many false hopes including the possibility of a Qantas flight to London I finally found a seat with Qatar going from Melbourne on Sunday 29th March and connecting on to Edinburgh! The downside was it would cost me £1,500 but on the positive side I would be going back to Scotland.

By this time there were only a few guests left in the hotel and it was planning on closing after I departed. I took the Skybus out to the airport and was horrified to see sitting a few rows ahead of me a young man who seemed to be sniffling and sneezing a lot. I kept my distance and made sure anything I touched on the bus was protected by my sanitized cloth. Despite having done an online check-in we had to join a queue for over two hours just to pick up our boarding cards. Beyond security everything in duty-free was shut. The A380 flight to Doha was full but the service was pretty good in difficult conditions. In some ways I had been spoilt on all my Emirates flights but I did not consider it to be fair to compare Qatar's service with theirs. When we got to Doha, the airport was very quiet and, much to my frustration, the duty-free shops were all closed. The airline had offered me the opportunity to upgrade to Business Class from which I would get Business Lounge access but at £700 extra. I reckoned I'd spent more than enough on this trip so I declined.

Back in Edinburgh I sped through arrivals and was delighted to find that there was an M&S store at the airport at which I could buy essential foodstuffs as I had nothing fresh in my flat. The final stage of my odyssey was trying to get from the airport back home to Glasgow. There was virtually no transportation operating except the airport bus to Edinburgh City which I took followed by a train to Glasgow and a taxi home.

My philosophy has always been to look forward to a positive future. With challenging times ahead I am really up for it in a quirky kind of way.